Boys Don't Cry

Tim Grayburn

H
**HODDER &
STOUGHTON**

First published in Great Britain in 2017 by Hodder & Stoughton

1

A CIP catalogue record for this title is available from the British Library

Hardback ISBN 978 1 473 63690 3
Trade paperback ISBN 978 1 473 63691 0
eBook ISBN 978 1 473 63692 7

Typeset in Electra by Palimpsest Book Production Ltd, Falkirk, Stirlingshire

Printed and bound by CPI Group (UK) Ltd, Croydon, CRO 4YY

Hodder & Stoughton policy is to use papers that are natural, renewable and recyclable products and made from wood grown in sustainable forests. The logging and manufacturing processes are expected to conform to the environmental regulations of the country of origin.

Hodder & Stoughton Ltd
Carmelite House
50 Victoria Embankment
London EC4Y 0DZ

www.hodder.co.uk

For Frank

'Mental illness is a fact of life that needs demystifying and destigmatising. Our aim with this show is to raise awareness of the fact that suicide is the biggest killer of men under 45 in the UK . . . men are struggling and they need all our help.'

Tim Grayburn, *Fake It 'Til You Make It*,
Edinburgh 2015

PART I

INTRODUCTION

Hi, I'm Tim.

[Pause]

I have chronic depression and acute anxiety.

[Pause]

This means that sometimes without my medication I can sink very deep and think about killing myself.

[Pause]

But it also means that most of the time I am perfectly happy and I forget it even exists.

[Pause]

I have recently begun to become proud of it.

Those words came out of my terrified mouth for the first time on a small stage at the Edinburgh Fringe Festival in 2014. I was standing in front of a hundred people and my girlfriend Bryony and I were there to see if we could make a theatre show about depression. It was only 11 months since I had first talked to Bryony about having depression. It was only 11 months since I had first really talked to anyone about having depression. Before that I had hidden my clinically diagnosed illness from everyone I knew because I didn't want people to think that I was a pussy. 'You've got what? Just get on with it, mate.' That was what I was terrified of hearing.

I had tried hard to 'just get on with it'. I had tried with lots of denial, lots of drink and drugs and lots of not coming to terms with or understanding what was happening to me.

Before I started to talk about my depression, my life involved sitting in an office in central London buying media for a big, arsehole, banking brand. I was single, commuting into work on the sweat freight number 38 bus and living in a shithole basement room with damp and mice as mates. Now, I've escaped that rat race and I am sitting at my desk with my son staring at me in confusion while his equally confused dad tries to figure out how to write a story about how his depression led him to co-write, co-perform and tour a theatre show around the world.

I guess the story begins with the unconditional, inquisitive, head-over-heels love of Bryony Kimmings and how it took that love to make me start to face up to the fact that I'd been secretly living with the fuckhead called depression for seven years. I'm going to throw up all sorts of stuff in this book, from how I almost decided to hang myself, to how I ended up sitting here alive and not dead writing a book. It took a series of events to happen for me to get here and I'm going to tell you all about them one by one – some of it is sad, some of it is soppy-soaked love sick on a page and some of it is full of hope and fun. Above all, I hope it will be helpful. Wisdom comes with age and experience; I'm only thirty-two but my younger twenty-five-year-old depressed and anxious self would have loved to hear the story of how I came to understand depression.

Nowadays I'm just a man who has decided to tell other men that you're not weak if you ask for help and I'd happily go toe to toe with any fella who says otherwise. My brain might be broken but my left hook ain't. An open mind is the only tool you'll need to learn and think differently and hopefully this book will encourage that.

CHAPTER ONE

B: *Depression? Was that word ever mentioned?*
T: *No, never, didn't have a clue what it meant.*

So I guess it'd be polite to introduce myself. For someone who's not a writer I've decided that that's the easiest place to start. I realise I'm no celebrity writing my autobiography but hearing about where I came from might help you get to know who I am and perhaps understand how my illness unfolded. To be honest, I'm kind of figuring it out for myself. Writing it all down for the very first time is making me think about things differently. It's making me try and see what I've done and become from a different perspective. For a while, I thought I'd try to frame the whole book in a kind of *Usual Suspects* back to front narrative and be really clever about it but I'm not clever. I'm thirty-two, six feet tall and covered in freckles. I was born in Durban, South

Africa, although I grew up in Oakley, a little village in Buckinghamshire. I'm the eldest of four children and my most prized possession is my son Frank. I love good people. I hate bad people. Something I always thought I'd do – drive around in a Ferrari like a twat. Something I never thought I'd do – write a book about my depression.

Apparently this isn't enough of a background story, so I've promised the editor I'd elaborate . . .

My mum and dad got married in April 1981 and three months later Dad got offered a job in construction out in South Africa. They decided that the lights of Lancaster weren't doing it for them any more so they figured they'd go for it and have an adventure. Two years after they first set up home there, I was born and their world exploded with happiness at the arrival of a mini superman/prophet. I don't remember anything about growing up over there – what I do remember comes from the photographs and home videos I've seen. I remember one video that was a classic camera tour of the house – everything looks eighties, my mum has glasses the size of a helmet wrapped around her face – like the ones Deirdre Barlow had in *Coronation Street* – and I'm running around in the garden with our dog Sam and it looks nice and peaceful. Other than that I have no real recollection of my life then. It baffles me when people say they remember being two years old – what is there to remember? Food, shitting, food and shitting. Surely they can't remember consciousness at that age – I struggle to remember how my brain worked yesterday. I do realise, though, that it's important to consider how you might have been emotionally as a child when you're trying to pull apart how you think and feel as an adult. I get it – it's important to figure out where it all started. My mum says I was just a normal little two-year-old boy; nothing alarming stood out. Mind you, unless there is a diagnosed illness or learning difficulty there wouldn't be much that would stand out in the behaviour of a two-year-old, I suppose – unless you started speaking Spanish or doing press-ups, or something. Apparently I was very sociable with all her friends' children and was quiet but happy. Because I was the first child and couldn't watch and learn from an older sibling, I pottered around, probably moving one toy to different spots of the house, back and forth all day long. I've seen it, that's what two-year-olds do – always busy, like an ant. So, I was just a normal toddler, by the sounds of it. However, last year I watched a home video of when I was around three or four and I did seem shy and full of questions. I wondered at the time, 'Was I a depressed, anxious little dude even then?' Maybe I had the same questions about the world then as I do now but I hadn't learnt the vocabulary to express them. Who knows what was going on in my head? Probably nothing other than pure joy in discovery.

As I say, I can't remember what life was like in South Africa but I'm sure that up until the arrival of my sister

Sarah there was a lot of food and shitting. Seg (Sarah Elizabeth Grayburn) was a little cave monster Bam Bam baby. She had a huge Afro from the off, which still can't be explained as she has DNA derived from two white parents. Again, from assessing the home videos, she looks like an adventurous, confident little girl who only sought fun and big legs of meat, like the little *Flintstones* character she reminds me of. She's in her thirties now and hasn't experienced clinical depression and hopefully never will. Is this because she was that sort of child? Are we born with depression? Is it a seed that's in there waiting to grow with the help of modern day living, stress, pain and hardship? As a doctor of absolutely nothing, I believe there are too many variables to pinpoint the exact cause of someone falling into a depression. The reasons why or how I got depressed were certainly never explained to me at the time – not like when I broke my arm playing football. 'This bone that you can see in this X-ray has a crack in it. After six weeks in a plaster, the crack will heal and you will be fixed.' I may not be a doctor but I am a human being – someone who has experienced and, so far, been lucky enough to live through an illness of the one organ we still don't know everything about. And it seems it's taken seven years of my life and six months of writing a book to get anywhere near the same closure I achieved after breaking my arm. It's funny how depression is usually associated with hardship or poverty or loss. I didn't have any of that and it happened to me. Robin

Williams didn't have any of that and it happened to him. Each case of depression is as individual as the people suffering from it – no one can judge or feel what someone else feels in his or her own head.

So, there we were, a British ex-pat family of four starting life in a continent where all human life had started. My dad worked in construction and practically built every home we've had with his bare hands. He's an old school man, a patriarch, a geezer. Good and bad connotations come with that tag. It's pretty glamorous being such a MAN. He's never used a washing machine, walks around with no top on and has a hammer in his right hand constantly. It's also quite sad because he's never really been allowed to open up. He's from that generation when it was unthinkable to talk about emotions and admit that you might feel sad or like watching ballet or show jumping. Or, at least, that's how I used to think of him. Since growing older, I've come to see that my emotional sensitivity has probably come from the old boy himself – he's tough on the outside but can be like candyfloss on the inside. He has his emotional triggers and one of his is his family. He will cry with pride, just as easily as he will cry when he feels his children's pain. It's just, I never witnessed it as a young boy – possibly I was sheltered from it for 'my own good', or perhaps I just didn't understand. Whatever the truth of that, there's no denying he was formed out of a Proper Northern Man mould. Once when he was tiling the roof of our garage in the middle of winter and he was wearing denim jeans he'd made into shorts (probably by ripping the legs off with his teeth), he came down at the end of the day walking like he was on stilts. He'd frozen his kneecaps. Like, proper frozen – they were dark blue – and when he walked there was a trail of dry ice behind him (there wasn't but it sounds better). Instead of being concerned about ever getting his knees back, he just walked around saying, 'Ice to meet you.' It's a miracle that the old boy is still alive. I think he's chopped off every one of his 10 fingers and regrown them like Wolverine. He once walked under some scaffolding and caught his head on a bolt that was sticking out. Some of his hair, skull and what looked like brain was left hanging from it. They had to staple it back up. But, before going to the hospital to check whether his brain had actually fallen out or not, he took a picture to send to me. Lad. All he eats is mayonnaise and butter and yet he manages to cycle 250 miles in one day. He's a miracle. He's the go-to man for anything that needs fixing and he's also the most protective leader a family could ask for.

My mum stayed at home to look after us kids while acclimatising to life in South Africa. She is a wonderful woman; she has a heart of a whale-sized lion – strong and so big that it has enough love for the planet. She's insanely creative and unquestionably selfless. She was a housewife and mum to us four kids (I'll introduce the other two shortly) for thirty years, but nowadays she's also a Police Community Support Officer. It's her first real career and she's perfect for it in the caring sense, though she's not much of a Sherlock Holmes. She comes home with a funny story after practically every shift. If she's not solving a neighbour dispute where they keep throwing vegetables at each other over the fence, she's making everyone cry with laughter regaling us with stories from the scene of the latest traffic bump or neighbourly dispute. One day she came home and told us that, earlier that day, a few police officers and firemen and herself were standing around assessing the damage after a car crash and they all looked down on the ground. There amongst the broken glass and skid marks was a pair of knickers (the skid marks were from the tyres). They all scratched their heads wondering how they could have got there. Only Ma knew. That morning, she'd slipped on her work trousers that were lying on her bedroom floor, not realising that her pants from the day before were still in the trouser leg. Out they came from the bottom of her trousers, straight on to the road at the crime scene. Not even Mr Holmes could have solved that one!

My dad is the head of the family in a practical sense but my mum is the head of the family in an emotional one, for sure. She's in tune with the happiness, sadness, joy and pain of all four of us kids. That's not to say that my dad isn't emotional because he is – he's more emotionally sensitive than Mum. He's a hard nut who likes a cry (he's gonna punch my head off). Mum's tough, she's in control of all of our feelings and kind of soaks up as much evil and pain as she can so we don't have to take the full brunt. I love them very much and I've been lucky enough to have them both around for the whole of my thirty-two years. Now that I'm a parent I can see just how hard both of them must have worked.

So I could have ended up living my whole life in South Africa but Mum and Dad decided that it had become too dangerous to stay. There were stories of handguns and handbags – pram-pushing mums having to carry weapons to protect themselves on the school run. It wasn't the life they had envisaged when they took the brave decision to up sticks from Lancaster to Durban. When I was four my dad was offered a job in Oxford so they decided to return and raise their family back in England. There was no need for guns in Oxford, just pens. Aside from Mum having to become Lara Croft, I do often wonder about what may have happened if we'd stayed there. Perhaps growing up by the beach in a warmer climate was my destiny, or maybe it wasn't. Perhaps I'd have been shot on my way to school? Perhaps I would have never suffered from depression. It's impossible to know, of course – I didn't stay and there's no knowing who I may have turned out to be. If you think about all the minutes of all the days of everyday life, surely there are an unquantifiable amount of life events that make you who you are and decide what you may be destined to suffer from. I've never been back to where I was born and, since I've become independent from my parents and can choose my own holidays, I've had a strange urge to return, to go back to where it all started. I don't know whether there'll be an answer there for me – probably not – but it would be nice to see it.

So we moved to a little village called Great Milton – just Mum, Dad, Seg and me. It was 1987 and I was just about to start school. I had a little twangy South African accent and I settled in pretty quickly. My first English friend was a twitchy, little tubbs. Twenty-nine years later Toby is still one of my best friends and he's been there for me, as I have for him, over the years when we've gone through hard times.

A few years went by and I was a normal, happy kid who ate bogeys and skateboarded like Bart Simpson (he was my hero). I was really happy. I remember this. I'm not just relying on the photo albums and home videos to know that I smiled a lot and felt real freedom in being who I was. I felt like a bird, free to explore everything the world had to offer. Of course, my whole world at that time consisted of various dens and playing tag, but I can remember skating and biking around the village with not a care in the world. And then my parents told me we were moving again. We were going to live on the other side of the county, which meant I had to move schools. I remember not wanting to go – I was a shy seven-year-old, for all the freedom I felt when I was in my comfort zone – and the thought of having to make new friends terrified me. What if there wasn't anyone who liked to skateboard and eat bogeys? Perhaps this was my first experience of anxiety? I remember going to the new school on a taster visit, to allow me to get my bearings, I guess. I remember standing behind the curtains and peering into the room where they were having their assembly. I scanned all the kids and felt scared and on edge. I wasn't raring to go and get stuck in, basically. I think Sarah was different – she was only five and hadn't been at our old school for very long, not long enough to make friends like I had. She probably bowled in there and got stuck in the mix immediately. I was more cautious and took a while to settle in. Luckily for me, shortly after I arrived there, I met the Nelson to my Bart – Andre. Andre was a chubby, happy kid who smiled all the time and had a mischievous side to him. He always had a pair of Kickers and I was well jealous – we could never afford them. Andre is my best mate to this day. We've gone through everything together, literally everything, and it's that track record I love to hang on to. It's important to me. I can't sit as comfortably in silence with anyone else in this world. One day when we're sitting side by side in piss-stained armchairs, Andre chained to his like Sloth from *The Goonies*, we'll be able to talk about all the shit we got up to and know we've been loyal friends since the day I moved to that school. We're so different and yet so similar that our friendship is untouchable. We support the same football team, we've grown up listening to the same music, and we've even had the same girl-friend. And yet, Andre will call a spade a spade and I will think about why it's called a spade. Sometimes I think he carries my happiness. Our history and our unspoken protection of one another is what defines us as mates. We've been there for each other through punch-ups and break-ups and we'll always have each other's back, no matter what.

I'm sure you're all dying to hear who the other two kids in my family are! I'm sitting here thinking, 'No one wants to know about this', which makes it hard to write. I've never liked talking about myself; I've been the kind of person who doesn't really talk unless I have to. But I've been given the opportunity to dribble out my thoughts and I shouldn't complain. Anyway, getting back to the point, my other two siblings are Jenny and Bobby. Jenny is bursting with talent and craziness in equal measure. She's very unique. She's got the heart of my mum and the guns of my dad, and if you cross her you know about it. I've always thought me and her are more alike, and Seg and Bobby are more similar. Bobby is the youngest and is ten years my junior. He's a proper chip off the old man. He loves building things and is very sensitive, always has been. When we were growing up, he used to cry whenever anyone had an argument. His sweet little soul was witness to a lot of family feuds and then he had a few of his own. As close as all of us are, a lot of feelings and disagreements are swept under the carpet to avoid those bastard feuds. All they need to know is that they are everything to me; along with Frank and Bryony, of course.

My parents didn't have a lot of money but we weren't necessarily poor. We had a good upbringing. They had their struggles bringing up four kids, like anyone else without a million-pound salary, and we now laugh at our once hillbilly ways. I had shit haircuts and clothes that were too small, mostly hand-me-downs. I was a huge Man United fan but I had to make do with last season's Newcastle shirt from my cousin every other year. I think my mum bought me some Peter Schmeichel shorts from a charity shop that I never took off. Half United, half Newcastle. I played like Cantona but looked like Beardsley. Andre always had the full United kit, including socks. I was the kid who never had Nike trainers or Walkers crisps in his lunch box but I had the best and most adventurous childhood anyone could ask for. That was thanks to my parents and their enthusiasm, and their ability to make fun out of anything and explore the outdoors. We had endless fields out the back of our house and we were one big, happy family. Most weekends my dad was working on the house and my mum was being a mum. We had complete freedom to roam about with all the kids from up our road and make dens and tree houses and explore acres of fields. In the summer we'd leave the house after breakfast, meet up with the others and then navigate our way back to one of our houses for a spot of lunch. We'd head back out with only a shout of 'Get back before it gets dark.' We'd just make it home, with one leg over the back-garden fence literally, as the sun rolled down the hill. It seemed as if life was going to be like that for ever.

CHAPTER TWO

B: I asked Tim his top three favourite things to do so you could get to know him a bit better. He said – playing football, eating dinner out and having sex. Classics!

Then, almost out of nowhere, I was sixteen. I had finished school and I had to make some choices about further education. If I had been asked what I thought about education I would have said, 'BORING.' I was only interested in people – in building relationships with friends and having as much fun as possible. Literally my only aim each day was to laugh so hard that a dribble of wee touched my Tommy Hilfiger, oversized boxers. I didn't have any concept of balance – 'work hard, play hard' was 'work as little as possible and then play like fuck until you are forced to work by an adult'. So, at sixteen I didn't know what I wanted to do. I didn't know who I was. I didn't really understand how important it was to get this next step in my life right in order to set up my future. I just kind of went along with whatever anyone around me said was good for me. I was too young to take any real responsibility for myself. Some kids have their heads screwed on tight at that age and some just don't. I was one of the ones that didn't. In fact, my head was so loose that I may as well have gone back to Year 7 and started secondary school all over again.

But, instead, I chose a subject for sixth form – Media Studies GNVQ Advanced, whatever that meant. My dad thought that I'd make a good sports journalist and journalism was part of the course and some of my close mates were going to do the same course, too, so I agreed. I couldn't make my own mind up so I just went along with what other people thought was best for me. With hind-fucking-sight I wish I had listened to my dad and gone down the journalism route after school because I do think it's something I may have been good at. Not so much the spelling and grammar part, but the inquisitive intrusive-ness part, bang on. But back then journalism sounded like accounting does to me now. I wanted to be a Footballer, an Actor or a Gangster. I didn't want a normal life. I wanted to see all sorts of things and do the things I was told I wasn't allowed to do. There was something just not quite right about going down the route of getting a secure job, buying a little house, having a wife and two kids, with *Bruce's Price is Right* on a Saturday night and keeping on top of the bills. I didn't want to settle into the Armchair of Norm and then die. (Ironically, that is kind of what I want now. Maybe swapping the *Price is Right* for *The X Factor*, or some other soul-sapping horseshit.) At the time, though, I wanted the best kind of life but I wanted it handed to me on a plate. I think if I'd been excellent at something I would have worked hard at it but I never was. I was just OK at everything. In a way it's nice that I was a dreamer and didn't want to settle for anything, but I also think perhaps being like that set me up for falling into depression in later life. When I realised that being a footballer, an actor or a gangster was a bit far fetched – after all, you can't just nab one of them down the Job Centre – maybe I started to panic. The panic may not have started until a few years later but I think that may have been when the seed was sown. For now, the seed of real life had only just been planted and I was still dreaming and pissing my pants on a daily basis.

I began to have a battle with my own thoughts at this time – who I wanted to be versus who I thought my parents wanted me to be. They were my idols, my gurus, the people I should listen to and hang on their every word. And I did. Except, I started to question certain things they said or the rules that they lived by, and wanted me to live by, but I didn't have the intelligence or confidence in myself to voice any opposing ideas. I was just trying to figure out what it all meant and I told myself off for questioning them and for even thinking that I might be different. I was a dreamer. I was a hippy kid who'd been born into a conservative family with a traditional conservative philosophy that I couldn't understand. I remember feeling angry towards them for stopping me from doing what other kids were allowed to do. They were pretty strict – I know it was purely because they cared and wanted to shelter me from all the badness out there but I had a chip on my shoulder about it. I guess in that way I was a typical teenager and I thought I knew better. As a parent now myself, I understand why they were strict but, back then, I got frustrated because I felt like I wanted to spread my wings and they were stopping me. I was always the one who had to be back from the pub before anyone else.

The pub in question was called The Royal Oak. It was in the village and I felt it was the best place for my wings to grow. It was an amazing place; there just aren't pubs like it any more. It was a real community. There were the old drunks, the posh married couple who sat and spoke politics while the kids were in bed across the road, the older kids who could drink legally (Andre's big brother and all his mates were among that crowd), us sixteen-year-olds pretending to be eighteen-year-olds, and the fourteen/fifteen-year-olds who smoked and played darts in the corner. It was our hub. It was where we went when we got into trouble with the kids from town and they used to drive into the village looking to beat us up. It was a village pub that was infamous around most of Oxfordshire. Everyone knew The Royal Oak. It's a derelict building now, boarded up with all its memories locked inside. It's a real shame – that sense of community left the day the pub died. RIP The Royal Oak.

So I was sixteen and I was trying to find my identity and starting to think I had a conflicting ideology from that of my family, mainly orchestrated or led by my dad. I had no idea what ideology, socialism or philosophy even meant back then but, looking back, this is when they started to become important to me without me even knowing it. I didn't go any further with those thoughts, though, I just smoked weed and chased girls. Basically, I made my priority growing up and doing fun things. I hadn't lost my virginity like most lads; I was waiting for 'the one'. I was a very romantic kid. I dreamt of the day when I would be madly in love and have lots of kids running around playing tag and telling me how much they loved me. Anyway, back to not losing my virginity. I was the latest starter of puberty in history – sixteen years old when I got my first pube. There was this girl at school who everyone fancied – the head girl, every school has one, someone who seems untouchable. She casually offered me a blowjob and then full-blown sex on the swings one day. I had to refuse because I had a baby dick with no hair. The next day the whole school knew that I had turned down a chance to make me The King

– the bitch told everyone and it swept through the school like wildfire. I had had the winning lottery ticket in my hand and I had burnt it. I didn't get bullied but there were a lot of laughs at my expense and it bothered me. I wanted to know when I was going to be able to be a man. I felt that I was being left behind and it made me insecure – as insecure as most sixteen-year-olds. Basically, I was a kind of popular kid with no pubes who loved playing football, listening to music and smoking weed; essentially, I was just like any other normal teenager.

I left school with hope and optimism for the future. I didn't know how my brain worked and I didn't even want to know but I decided to go to uni because I was told that I'd have to get a job if I didn't. I wasn't ready for a job – I hadn't even had sex yet, or taken my first ecstasy, been to a club, travelled to a European city with mates, had a fight, or fallen in love. I wanted to do all of that 1,000 times first and THEN start to think about what job I should have for the rest of my life. Naive as it was, I think most kids were thinking the same. I saw my first job as the end of my life. I just wasn't ready to throw in the towel. After very little research into universities and the courses they had to offer, I fell back on the old, trusted Media Studies and hatched a plan to go to what-ever uni would accept me. A mate and I agreed that we'd only go to a uni that accepted us both – we were too wimpish to go it alone. In the end, Chichester was the only place that accepted us and, without even going to visit, we signed up.

Just around the time I was packing up to leave home for the first time, on 2 October 2000, I heard some terrible news. Danny, one of the guys who was part of the older lot of lads from the village, committed suicide. He was just twenty-two years old. He was part of the furniture in The Royal Oak; he was one of the people who protected us from outsiders. It ripped right through the middle of The Royal Oak and village community. He hung himself from a tree at the bottom of the playing field; he didn't leave a note. It shook us all badly. I didn't know Danny very well but a friend of mine called Nick did. Nick and Danny were like me and Andre – they were joined at the hip. Nick found him in that tree along with four of the other lads. As one of Nick's best mates now I can say that day changed him for ever. Of course it would. I've just called him and asked him if he minds if I include Danny in the book. He said, 'I'm not very good at talking about it, mate.' It upsets me that he had to go through that. It upsets me that Danny didn't feel like he could talk to anyone. And it upsets me to think of all the collateral damage that day has caused – his dad, his brother, Nick and all the other people I don't know who were close to him. I asked Nick if he was offered any therapy at the time to help him deal with it and he replied, 'Nothing was offered. I just learnt to get on with it.' What kind of planet do we live on where it is acceptable for a twenty-two-year-old lad to be left to get on with it and figure out what had just happened all on his own? I remember after the funeral we did the things that help us grieve – we talked about all the good times and recounted funny stories. I don't remember a lot of support being offered and I don't remember talking about it seriously. I know some people don't like to talk and Nick is one of those people. He's very strong willed and he manages, but I can't help but think if as a younger man he'd been encouraged to talk about it all and have some closure with a professional, then maybe it would have benefited him. And, of course, the same goes for Danny. What if he had been able to talk? What if he were a twenty-two-year-old now – would he have felt able to talk about his problems? Unfortunately we can't know the answer to that question. What I do think is fascinating is that I feel worse thinking about what happened to Danny now, than I did when it happened sixteen years ago. It's because I know, to some extent, what he must have been going through. I understand. Back then I didn't. I didn't have a clue. To have compassion for the mentally ill, do you need to experience it yourself first? Maybe. It's certainly impossible to understand what depression and suicidal thoughts feel like unless you've experienced them yourself – it's like a dude trying to understand how painful childbirth is. But perhaps you can still have empathy. To put Danny's pain in perspective you just have to think that he preferred death to his suffering, whatever it was. No one knew for sure that he had depression but it is the most likely answer.

It was my first exposure to suicide and the world of mental illness. I have to be honest, though; I said my goodbyes on the day of his funeral and just got on with being seventeen. I didn't know it then but Nick would end up being there for me when I fell into my first bout of depression. Maybe subconsciously he wasn't going to let it happen again.

I went to uni and dived right in. I lost my virginity on the very first night and I can't remember her name – not because I'm a bad person, but because I have a terrible memory. It's quite sad that the romantic kid in me had been defeated by the macho pressures of 'getting your end away'. I always imagined my first would be my last. Fuck me, I'm glad it wasn't, though. Not because she wasn't worth it – she was – but because I think it's important to have lots of partners until you find the right one. Some people are lucky and find the right one on the first throw of the dart. For me, like most of us, I continuously find the right one until life and time and experience proves otherwise. Anyway, uni was amazing. Chichester was quiet and Bognor Regis, for those who don't know, is a seaside town with a campus slapped in the middle of it. I don't want to offend the Bognorites, because I loved the place, but it was a shithole. A classic British seaside town whose glory days were well behind it. We didn't care, though; as long as there was alcohol, music and friends we thought we were in Utopia. No parents to give us a curfew, clubs and house parties to go to every night of the week and – plain and simply – the ability to get up to mischief. I still wasn't interested in academic learning, just real-life learning. My attendance in lectures and tutorials was poor and when I did make it, I usually just fell asleep or drew pictures of cocks on the desks. I wasn't a complete rebel, though, and there was perhaps 5 per cent of me that began to be concerned about my future and what I was going to do about getting a job when uni was over. I struggled with the work – I struggled to trust my own opinion and I never put my hand up in case my answer sounded stupid. I was terrified of being called thick or being laughed at, so I pretended that I either didn't care or that I knew everything. I just scraped through. Unlike my lack of confidence in myself, as a young man in my late teens I always had confidence that, whatever happened in life, it would all be all right. In the years that followed, I lost that belief but today, as I write this, I've just about got it back. For me it's a very important part of keeping myself mentally healthy – a kind of blind faith that I'll be all right no matter what life throws at me. It interrupts my alternate anxious reality that it could end up not being 'all right'. As a teenager, it was my laidback attitude to life that let me think everything would be all right in the end – nowadays I have to work on feeling like that. I get there, not because I'm laidback, but because I work hard to feel mentally well and happy. At eighteen, though, I was pretty sheltered from all the evils of the world and, during those three years at Chichester, I was in a sort of ignorant bliss, where every Tuesday night I'd dress up as a cheerleader and drink snakebite, shit my pants and wake up in a bin. I may have been eighteen but I was no adult, believe me.

I graduated – just. I got a 2:1 – at least, that's what my CV says. I actually got a 2:2. I missed out by 1.64 per cent, or something ridiculously close like that, so in my mind I got a 2:1. I apologise to Maxus who gave me a job on the basis of my 2:1 but, to be fair, you did only get me in for an interview 'because you'd heard that I was a lot of fun' so maybe you can forgive my little white lie. After I threw that weird hat in the air, I decided that I still wasn't ready to get a job – I was going to go travelling. My efforts to discover who I was and what I wanted to do with my life had failed miserably at uni, so I thought perhaps travelling might provide the answers. Plus, the thought of doing what I did at uni but without the lectures for a whole year appealed. Six years earlier, Andre had been expelled from school for smoking weed. (Silly really – expelled for smoking a plant that grows from the earth? It was naughty, sure, but expelling him? Bit much, I thought.) He went straight to work and hadn't had a chance to piss around at uni like I had so when I told him I was going to go travelling he was well keen to go with me. I moved back home and we worked all summer and booked our tickets to go at the end of October 2004. That summer of working together was the perfect warm-up for our travels. Me, Andre and another friend of ours Stav – the three amigos, as we cringingly called ourselves – were inseparable. We did everything together. We basically worked, chilled in the week and lived for the weekend when we could go out and drink and chase girls. Pretty soon, Stav decided he wanted to go travelling, too. He thought he'd leave before us and the plan was to hook up in Australia. When the time came we said our goodbyes to Stav and patiently waited our turn. I wanted a 'round the world' experience because I thought it literally meant I would see everything there was to see in the world if I went from Thailand to New York in a year. Bless my stupid self. My itinerary included Thailand, Australia, New Zealand, Fiji, LA, San Francisco and New York. That was quite a big trip for an eighteen-year-old jizz ball. At the time I had only been to Spain, Greece, Malta, Amsterdam and Morecambe, so it was a big deal. Andre just booked a ticket to Australia, as he was keen to work and live there for a bit. Even though I hated the idea of being on my own for any of the trip, I still wasn't keen to work so, very unlike myself, I stuck with the world ticket. I couldn't wait to get going because, aside from all the fun I was going to have, I genuinely thought I would meet some mystical Buddha who would tell me the next steps I needed to take to lead a fulfilled and successful life.

We ran out of money three months into the trip. Our solution was to get a job on a banana farm. Andre and I were picked up from a backpackers' hostel in Cairns and driven out to a hillbilly ranch a couple of hours away. We handed our passports over as a security deposit because we had no money to pay for the first two nights' rent. We were told that after our first week's pay we could get it back. There was no alternative. The ranch was a dark, dingy, brick-walled, garage-like hellhole. It was a dump; our beds looked like the sheets hadn't been changed for twelve years and there was a fucking emu walking through the room and shitting wherever it fancied. I could smell the exploitation of young naive backpackers in the air and I knew immediately that I wasn't going to last long. I lasted one day. In the morning, we were sent to different farms and Andre lucked out. He got to leave at 7am, half an hour later than I did. At 6:30am, a bunch of us got on to the back of a tractor and were driven into a field. We had no idea what we were getting ourselves into. The banana field was a swamp pit with rats and snakes all over the place. We weren't given wellies, so our feet were almost submerged in shit. We were told to place ourselves under a bunch of bananas, not a bunch like you get in Sainsbury's but a King Kong-sized bunch that weighed about 50 kilos, and then the local Aussie bullies cut the bunch at the top and we'd have to take the weight, walk through the swamp and load it on to a truck. Every bunch had a protective canopy around it to keep the rats away, but they weren't exactly the Fort Knox of the banana world. Every bunch was full of rat piss and one even had a family of rats still in it while it was on my shoulder; they ran out down my arm and into the swamp. 'Fuck this,' I thought. When I got back to the prison ranch at 7pm Andre was sitting on the sofa with his feet up, watching TV and smoking a cigarette. He took one look at me and laughed. I was covered in shit, head to toe. He really had lucked out – he'd been given wellies, shoulder pads and basically just had to walk around his farm cutting down leaves with a machete. I told him I was getting out of there. Andre said it was easy money for him and he wasn't as precious as me about sleeping in beds where people had died. He was staying. The owner of the farm wouldn't give me back my passport until I gave him the rent money. I only had $40 in my pocket so I used $20 to get the next bus back to civilisation and the other $20 for food, some fags and a drink, and left my passport behind. Not exactly Bear Grylls but it's what I needed at the time. I didn't have any idea what I was going to do but I always thought/hoped that something would pop up. It did. I arrived back in Cairns at about 9pm and it was just getting dark. I sat in the park on a picnic bench with all my belongings and started to panic, thinking that I might have to sleep rough. Then, out of nowhere, three Canadian guys called Seb, Blake and Alex came up to me and offered me a beer. I told them what had happened and the situation I had got myself into. They said they'd all chip in and pay a week's rent at their hostel for me, get me a job with them landscape gardening in the morning and then I should have enough money to pay them back, get my passport and pay for the following week's rent. The money landscape gardening was three times as much as the banana slavery and I ended up working there for two months, making enough money to keep travelling. It was experiences like that that were good for me, in terms of listening to my instincts, but I knew that I couldn't count on having a career as a flukey bum.

It was one of the best years of my life, a total joyous fucked-up adventure but, if anything, it confused me even more about what I wanted to do with my life. It was such a valuable experience in my development as a human but, at the time, it didn't solve anything in terms of cementing my future. Being away for so long set me up for a fall when I did return home to real life. I loved being on the move and not knowing what I was doing the next day, but you can't live like that in the twentieth-century real world can you? At least, that's what I had been taught.

I had done uni, I had done travelling and now I had run out of excuses to avoid work. While I was travelling in Australia, I had hooked up with a girl I'd met on a family holiday when I was sixteen. She was my first love and when I say love, I mean love. It annoys me when people say to youngsters, 'You don't know what love is.' Well, I did. Falling in love is the same whether you're eighteen or eighty. Only you can know how it feels to you. It's a fascination and a subconscious gravitational pull towards that person. All you want to do is lie as close to them as possible and kiss and be consumed by them. I don't think it can be fully explained why we love, we just do. We don't choose; it's chosen for us. Every time I've fallen in love, it has happened subconsciously and under instruction from my inner cupid. I met Laura for the first time around a pool table in Rhodes. I was from Oxford and she was from Birmingham. I abandoned my siblings and she abandoned the friend who had come with her and her parents on holiday. We swam in the sea and held hands and kissed for approximately sixteen hours a day. Cute. When we got back to the UK I had started getting the National Express up the M40 to spend my weekends with the person who I thought was The One. I did this every week for six months or so with my buzzing balls and naive romantic brain. It didn't last long. We split up because, frankly, it was a pain in the arse and we were both missing out on the fun to be had on our own home soil. We stayed in touch, though, and we met up every now and again while we were at university. I found out she was going to be in Australia at the same time as I was and so we hung out together there. We decided to go on to New Zealand and Fiji together as an official couple. I travelled on to North America on my own, while she went to South East Asia. When we got back to the UK her parents moved to Spain so I did the honourable thing and upped sticks to Kidderminster to live with her. I hated it. I was living away from all my friends and family and I didn't want to miss out, but the urge to be by her side kept me there. I had no car, because I couldn't afford one, and all I did have was an old bike that didn't ride properly. We had no money and Kidderminster wasn't exactly an economic boom town full of jobs for graduates. But we had each other. I got a job working in a factory putting together machinery on a line with a fifty-five-year-old called Sid, who was the person closest to me in age but nowhere near in interest. I remember feeling low throughout this time but not depressed. To mix it up we moved to Bristol – she'd got her dream job and, once again, I was left to find any old job that I could. I was lost in this new world of responsibility because I didn't have a map of life written for me to follow. I didn't know what I wanted to do and I didn't really know who I was. Because of my degree, I looked in the papers for job titles that had the word 'Media' in them – that's how clueless I was. I finally got a job that didn't involve talking about tits all day with Sid. I was to be a Media Planner/Buyer, whatever that meant, for a small agency in Thornbury just outside Bristol. The guy who ran the company was a lovely, gentle man of wisdom who had been and done it all in

London and thought he'd do it on his own in the countryside. Fair play.

So Laura and I both had good jobs and were living in Bristol. Good times. I was madly in love with the girl – we had the romantic history and we were discovering this shit adult life together away from both of our home towns. And then the gloves came off. One night she came back from an evening out with her mates. I was asleep in bed, and she woke me up spoiling for a fight. She was extremely jealous, although she had no reason to be. She woke up the next morning full of regret and apologies. I dished out the warning that if it ever happened again I would pack up and leave. She nodded like a little child who'd been told they're dangerously close to losing their favourite toy. Two nights later, the same thing, sleep victim once again. I packed my car the next morning and I never saw her again. The love gods had lied to me.

CHAPTER THREE

T: I was around twenty-four/twenty-five, can't exactly remember when but something changed completely in me, I just woke up different. I didn't want to hang around with my mates any more, I didn't want to do things I loved doing like playing football and seeing friends. I just thought, 'I'm tired and I just need to deal with it myself.'

I was back at my mum and dad's heartbroken and with no idea of what direction to go in terms of a career. Things weren't going as easily as I thought they might. My attitude was, 'Fuck it – I'm going to raise hell, in that case.' I had to get out of my parents' house and live with friends and get in the mix. It seemed like a solution but really I was just taking myself out of one situation and putting myself into another with no real purpose or direction. I moved into a brand new flat with Andre and

Stav on the Cowley Road in Oxford. I had to get over Laura asap so I slept with the estate agent. Lad. He wasn't a lad; she was a twenty-two-year-old blonde, lovely female. We were all so excited about what this year might bring. We were finally living together – our house, our rules. It was time to blanket my thoughts, feelings and emotions with lots of fun. We had a year of real debauchery – drinking, drugs, sex and lots of rock and roll. It's massively embarrassing but us three and Chris LC (another best mate) pretended we were in a band to get more attention from girls. It worked. We were young and horny, getting girls and as many as possible was our number one aim. Ten years later, I'm ashamed but I also know that it's part of growing up and I will never regret the fun that we had. I just regret not having the capacity to balance the fun with some practical actions that might have helped me become a responsible, mentally strong adult.

I was working in a media agency just outside of Oxford during the day – they were the self-proclaimed largest UK media agency outside of London – and, to begin with, I really enjoyed it. I knew in the back of my head that it wasn't me, though – I was just doing it because it was a job. Andre, meanwhile, had an engineering job at Cullum Science Centre putting together thermometers, or something. He basically slept in his car all day playing a tennis game on his phone. One day he went the toilet at 10am, pulled his pants down, sat on the toilet resting his hard hat against the toilet wall and woke up three hours later without anyone noticing that he was gone. The lunchtime bell had woken him up. He then got in his car for his lunch break and fell asleep until a colleague tapped on his window at 4pm and said it was time to go home. He did nothing there but loved it. Stav was a professional golfer and made good money teaching; he always had a good work ethic. He didn't want to do it, but he never moaned and always got up and went in to work – probably because it was a lot more interesting than what we were doing.

They were in the same boat as me and their future was as insecure as mine, but they were able to park the anxiety and I wasn't. It started to creep from the back into the forefront of my mind and, the truth is, I was extremely vulnerable to depression at this time and my lifestyle probably pushed me right into the deep end of it. On the other hand, it may have happened to me even if I'd lived like a monk, who knows? Looking back now, though, this is when the depression slowly started to creep in.

I acted like every day was my last, like a rock star without any talent or money. I slept around, got aggressive, had fights, drank more, did more drugs, and tried to fight any negative thoughts off in all the wrong ways. The problem was I didn't know how to equip myself with all the right tools to slay them. In school we hadn't been told the fact that there was a one in four chance you will suffer from a mental health problem, or that one day you might have an illness that will whisper suicidal thoughts in your ears. If I'd known at the time, I wouldn't have acted like a fake, knobhead rock star. I would have told my family, my friends and my doctor the truth about how I was feeling and learnt how to accept who I am. I would probably have been diagnosed much sooner and then would have been able to focus on getting myself better.

But it wasn't just my lack of knowledge about the illness that was stopping me from speaking up, it was the thought that everyone would think that I was a wimp. 'Get on with it', 'life is hard' – I didn't want the stigma of being someone who couldn't cope. I didn't want people to laugh behind my back. You hear about depression daily nowadays but it wasn't spoken of then. The word wasn't associated with an illness like it is now; it was more of an insult. The definition of 'stigma' in the Oxford Dictionary is: A mark of disgrace associated with a particular circumstance, quality, or person. I didn't want to fall into that category. I didn't want to be a disgrace. I wanted to be normal, to fit in. Let's face it, when you're in your twenties, the number one thing that most of us want to do is have FUN. It is a time of complete freedom from your parents and it's an opportunity to do what the hell you like. The thought of opening up about my depressive thoughts to a group of twenty-five-year-olds seemed like a sure-fire way to exclude myself permanently from a decade of fun. So I didn't. Depression can be hidden in happiness and that's exactly what I did. Fun was the only thing that kept me away from the pitch-black darkness in my head that I faced when I was alone. I know now that trying to blanket what I was feeling in a duvet of drink, drugs and debauchery was the exact opposite of what I should have been doing. I wish I had dealt with it head on and tried to get myself better before I let the depression completely move in. Depression was busy hanging pictures on the walls of my skull; if I'd just accepted it and talked about it with someone – anyone – perhaps it could have just temporarily visited. And then I could have politely shown him the door out of my life.

The germ of depression started with asking myself the unanswerable questions – 'What is life all about?' 'Who am I?' (Said like Derek Zoolander.) When I was coming to the end of living in the flat with Andre and Stav, I'd act like everything was fine but, whenever I was on my own, I'd sit and think about everything, usually all the way through the night, fuelling my insomnia. It's hard to dig around in my memory of how it felt back then because it was so dark that I filtered those experiences and feelings straight to the recycle bin. I didn't ever want to talk about it and I never thought I would have to bring it all up again. I was a happy boy and then a happy teenager; I was expecting to be a happy man. Why would I not be? I remember thinking, 'Well, life's shit isn't it?' That thought was the little match to the wick of my depression bomb. Instead of talking about why I thought life was shit, I just pretended that life was amazing. I thought life was shit because I didn't understand the purpose of it – do you just live and then die? Who put me here? If there is a god, why do we have history books full of disasters? Why is the world so unfair? Why do some people have it all and others have nothing? Why are my experiences so limited to this planet, this country, this town, this village, this house, this head? These questions were unanswerable at the time; some of them still are, of course. So I was never going to get an answer. But it meant that I stayed up all night, lying in bed pleading for the questions to stop so I could get some sleep. I became an insomniac and, with that, everything started to deteriorate. You probably won't find this on the NHS website but it's official – having no sleep drives you mental.

And then I got angry. Why weren't other people as pissed off as me? Confusion turned to anger, anger to sadness, sadness to despair. All of these emotions and feelings were mixed in my head like prawns in a Pad Thai. Every now and then one of them would pop up from the noodles of nine-to-five life. So while my days were full of fun and discovery, my nights alone were full of suicidal thoughts. I had an amazing decade in my twenties, but if I had just been more honest about how I felt, if I had been able to talk about my thoughts and fears, if Mr Stigma Fuck wasn't around to stop me, I know that those suicidal thoughts wouldn't have been a part of it.

A normal day was like this:

08:00 – Alarm goes off. I struggle to get up because I have only really just fallen asleep after being woken up at 04:00 by the thoughts in my head. But the world wants me up at this time so I just have to do it.

08:59 – Arrive in the work car park. Deep breaths in my car while still trying to wake myself up. Am riddled with dread at the thought of having to convince my bosses that I give a shit about making money when four hours earlier I was asking myself who made the universe.

13:00 – Lunchtime. I pretend I'm going to the shops when, really, I drive around the corner and into a field to try to sleep in my car. I put the seats down and shut my red eyes, desperately trying to get some energy from somewhere. I never manage to sleep.

15:30 – Try to balance a conversation with nice people who have no idea what is going on in my head with what is actually going on inside my head. Then I politely say, 'Excuse me' and scurry to the bogs. Cry in the toilets.

17:00 – Drive home. The whole thirty-minute journey home I laugh to myself with confusion about why I am crying.

18:00 – I walk in the front door like I've just had the best day of my life. I sit with my two best mates and drink and laugh it all away.

02:00 – Pass out.

04:00 – The Ghost of Depression and his questions wake me up to remind me that it's about to start all over again.

Obviously this wasn't every day. Saturdays and Sundays I didn't have the work. And I didn't cry every day – on average, once a week, maybe. And all the while, I had a great life on paper. I played sports, kept fit, had good, solid best mates – proper ones who take the piss until there's nothing left but who'll be there in a second when things get ugly.

I had just turned twenty-five and, like all good things, our time at Cowley Road was coming to an end. We couldn't afford to live another year like the one we just had – financially, emotionally and physically it would be impossible. We were all going to have to move back home to our parents' houses. We desperately didn't want to but it served us right for blowing our beans in the first year of true independence. I don't think we would have been allowed to stay in that flat even if we had wanted to. The landlord and the neighbours were so fed up with us that, once we were gone, they must have thrown a similar party to the ones we had every night.

And then I slowly started to fall apart. I felt like I wasn't actually living in my own body and that someone else was behind the wheel. I didn't know what anxiety was at the time but I know now that this is when it took control of me. Now I wasn't just dealing with depression, but anxiety had joined the shit party: a double dose of crapness. It really was a horrible time. I felt like I wasn't meant to be here; that I wasn't wired up right for this planet. I didn't face up to any of these feelings, though. I brushed them under the carpet every day. This went on for so long that eventually things started happening that brought alarm to the people around me.

I started getting in a few fights. We went on a night out and some idiot starting threatening a girl mate of mine because she wasn't interested in his drunken bird-call. He was just about to grab her by the throat, so I punched him and broke a knuckle in my right hand. He scattered off and I thought that would be the last time I'd see him. Three or four hours later, though, we were walking up the street and he came out of the alleyway and had a swing at me. He completely missed so we started to chase him. He was looking over his shoulder and then BANG he ran straight into a lamppost and knocked himself out, smashing out a few teeth with it. Good. He deserved it. But these scraps started to happen more often. I may have never started them, but I never did anything to avoid them either. I'd say I'm still a fiery character if wronged but, nowadays, I'll avoid aggro as much as I can and that's because I'm moving closer to knowing who I am and being comfortable with who that is. Back then, I was fighting my way out of a corner that I felt I'd been dumped into by the pressures of the world. I believe behind every violent person there's a good psychological reason for that violence. It's no excuse, of course, but no person is violent just for the hell of it, there's some history or serious insecurity behind it.

Not long after my hand had recovered from that punch, Andre and I went to play a game of squash. After I beat him (probably), we skipped the pub and got into my car to head home. It was pissing down and it was dark. I felt fine, though. In fact, I felt better than I had done the whole rest of the day, having done a good forty minutes of exercise. We set off with the stereo on, probably Snoop Dogg or Bob Marley, and it was on loud. I remember the noise really bothering me and then, as we got three miles into our journey back home, we approached a windy bit of country road. Andre was trying to talk to me over the music and, all of a sudden, everything around me seemed to become a war zone. A simple drive had turned into what felt like a car chase through a battlefield. Every sound was amplified by a thousand and I felt like my vision was on fast forward. My senses had taken on too much and I lost control of my actions. I put my foot down on the accelerator but not intentionally; I was a passenger now, too. Andre said, 'Slow down, kid' but it was too late and we aquaplaned over the waterlogged road. We smashed into the verge at about 70mph and came to a stop around 80 feet away from where we had first hit. I remember a lot of banging around like I was on a fairground ride and then it stopped. The police said the car must have rolled six or seven times to get to where we ended up. We landed on the wheels, the roof was flattened, the boot was smashed in and most of the windows were shattered. Our gym bags were nowhere to be seen – they were found the next day flung into the field on the opposite side of the road. It was a mini miracle that Andre was completely unharmed, not a scratch; I just had a little bit of glass in my left hand that had to be operated on but nothing serious. I remember when it was over being hunched down because of the roof and asking Andre if he was all right. 'I think so,' he said. He asked me the same and I nodded. We then climbed out and had a cigarette while we took it all in.

That was the first time my illness could have killed me. If it weren't for our seat belts, we wouldn't have survived. Was the panic attack spontaneous? No, I don't think so. I think it was a build-up of unrecognised, unattended-to symptoms of anxiety that I had been experiencing for a few months. At the time I didn't know what was happening to me in that car. I didn't know what anxiety meant and I didn't want to explain how I felt, in case my licence was taken away from me or in case the police, my parents, Andre and my mates all looked at me like I was crazy.

And still no alarm bells rang in me. It was just an accident that could have happened to anyone. What it really was, though, was a cry for help that no one could hear. I started shutting myself away from everyone. I just couldn't face normal life conversations; they bored me. I had questions in my head about whether I wanted to live or die so talking about the boring details of someone's day at work didn't interest me at all. The thing I didn't realise is that no one else knew this was how I felt. How could they? I had all my thoughts safely locked away in my ashamed brain vault of secrets. This, then, must have made me seem like a right arsehole. I wasn't; I was just so confused and lost and felt so alone. The only person who knew how I was feeling was my dog Maisy. It sounds mad but, I'm telling you, she knew. She felt my pain and tried every non-verbal trick in the book to let me know that she understood. I used to walk with her around the fields where I grew up and cry about the way my life was turning out. I hated myself; I had failed to discover happiness. I didn't think I had the rest of my life to keep going. For some reason I believed reaching 25 and not being successful meant that I had a lifetime of misery ahead. As each walk went by I was totting up the reasons for and against living. I felt my life was a shambles. I didn't know about love and kindness and nature and the true meaning of happiness. I didn't know about anything and I was giving up.

To make things worse, with no real plan in place, I quit my job. I hated being stuck inside the office and there was a little voice telling me that I needed to get out. 'That life you never wanted is happening to you right now; you need to get out before it's too late.' Being back at my mum and dad's made the symptoms of depression start to rise to the surface and now I had no job either. I felt extremely worthless, unconfident, fatigued and my insomnia was out in full force. It wasn't a good environment for me to be in but, at the same time, deep down, I did want to be close to my family. But they were so far away from understanding what was happening to me and I resented them for it, even though I never explained what I felt in detail. I did odd jobs for cash, labouring, roofing or working at festivals and then continued to go out and drink and piss around. I enjoyed myself when I was off my face but I was pretty miserable in the build-up to getting there and the next day, of course, was even worse. Alcohol seems to be your best friend and your worst enemy at the same time when you're suffering from depression. He's there through the good times but the next day, or even a few days later, he's nowhere to be seen, he's off befriending someone else whilst he waits for your return. When you're at your most vulnerable he'll slip back in and get you to forget all your problems and responsibilities. I realise now that at this time in my life alcohol was certainly more of an enemy than a friend. All I wanted to do was run away and, since then, this has been something I constantly battle with – an urge to run away and go where no one can find me. I wish I didn't have this feeling but I do.

It makes me hate myself for being so blinkered as to what is here in front of me, but I'm also happy that I'm not content with this modern life. I do dream of sun and beaches and humans enjoying life as nature intended – basically everyone just chilling the fuck out a bit – and I don't think there's anything wrong with that. It's no different to a kid dreaming of being a professional footballer.

After a few months, I was offered an alternative to living at home. I make it sound like home was some evil sort of prison, it wasn't. It was the safest place for me to be and it was a real home, no comfort like it. It's just that it was in the middle of nowhere. It was no place for a twenty-five-year-old bloke trying to figure shit out. A friend's mum lived in Spain and I think she got so fed up with me moaning about wanting to run away that she suggested I go and live out there for a while to see if I could find whatever it was I was looking for. It turns out that all that was out there was working on a building site and getting even more lost. Just before I left to go, though, I woke up and felt the previous few months of feeling miserable hit me all at once. It was a conclusive punch in the face of proper sadness. Before then I had always considered myself a fun, optimistic, person who'd say cocky stuff like, 'Nothing fazes me, mate.' Don't get me wrong, I know that struggling with adulthood is the same story for most kids – life's a piss take and then you're on your own – but this wasn't just a bit sad. The punch in the face hurt. It was like an internal vacuum cleaner sucking my soul away, drawing my face in and bagging up my personality. After a month in Spain, I flew back home a certified loser. I had worked in a restaurant and on a building site but spent every penny going out and getting drunk and then waking up with a hazy, don't care attitude.

The quick fix of drink or drugs or sex wasn't really doing it any more – maybe sex was still doing it a little bit. I needed something else, though, but I had no idea what it was. Back at home and trampling through the fields near our house with our dog Maisy, I walked past a tree we used to play at when I was a kid called the treehouse tree – the wonderful creative minds of eight-year-olds, eh? – and I thought that if I were going to hang myself then that would be where I'd do it. This was my first suicidal thought. It wasn't conclusive in any way and I was lucky enough to fight it enough to convince myself not to actually do it. But just the fact that I'd even thought about it made me even more confused and upset. I looked into Maisy's eyes for ages after that and thought about the possibility that she may be depressed, too, and, if she were, she wouldn't even have the capability to hang herself – she just had to keep going and live her life until old age takes it away. Maybe she's living her life to protect mine – her being there made me feel the love that she had for me and made me think that maybe that was my purpose, to

protect someone else from pain, whatever theirs might
be. I was saved by a dog.

Nothing was wrong, except for all of it; it wasn't
enough. I didn't have a problem with girls, my parents
were together, I had three beautiful siblings, I went on
nice holidays and I was twenty-five. I wanted the big
questions answered but, as I had been told by my parents
for my whole life, I want never gets. Maybe if I'd had
that amazing teacher when I was at school, like the ones
you see in films, who puts their hand on your shoulder
and says, 'Son, I think you are destined to study philosophy', I would have gone, 'Oh, OK' and discovered a
purpose to my life. I wouldn't have been so stupid with
my GSCE brain and tried to ignore the questions.
Anyway, the point is that something was happening to
me and I didn't know what it was. I'd never heard about
depression – that word didn't mean anything to me.
Whatever it was that I had, it certainly wasn't any illness
that I knew about. The daily fatigue, the loss of appetite,
crying, insomnia and the headaches were just something
I thought I had to cope with because I wasn't put together
as well as other people How was I supposed to know that
these were all symptoms of depression and acute anxiety?
I'd never heard about them in school. I wasn't a doctor.
I didn't study medicine. I did know, however, that I was
ashamed of them, especially the fatigue and crying. In
my world, boys weren't supposed to cry and they should
never moan about being tired. I didn't want everyone to

know about or hear me moaning about life. People around me only ever spoke of positive things, me included. I acted like I was at the top of my game. Years later, when I finally told a mate about how I had been feeling, he said, 'I thought you were the one who had it together more than any of us.' Just proves how much of an act I was putting on at that stage of my life. I didn't associate my symptoms with an illness; I was just a shit human. That was what I thought, and what I told myself.

So I had no idea what was happening to me and neither did my poor parents. I remember my dad coming up to my room and catching me crying to myself and he must have felt so helpless. He asked me what the matter was and I wasn't able to tell him. 'I don't know what's happening to me, Dad.' He started to cry as well and gave me a big hug. He wasn't equipped with the knowledge I have now about mental health because he wasn't taught about it. If it ever happens to my son I hope I'll know what to do to get him on a road to recovery as soon as possible; at least I'll know how to try to help with what I've learnt through my own experiences. But it shouldn't just be people who have experienced depression themselves who can help. Everyone should know what to look out for – we should be taught about it in school, like First Aid for the brain. We need to seek out the sufferers – not just rely on them to make the first move. Sufferers or former sufferers have a dog sense of smell for depression and can sniff it out with ease. It's also practically impossible to begin to tell someone that you're depressed – all the shame, loneliness and despair makes it seem like a last resort. You don't want to become a burden or make someone think that they have to fix you. Maybe that's why the physical symptoms of depression are there – the sad face, the dropped shoulders and the low tone. They're all a cry for help, an advert saying, 'Please talk to me because I can't even begin to start this conversation.' I spot it everywhere I go now – at work I can see who is in the same boat, and the same goes for friends and even people I see on the train. As much as we need to be there for depressives, to let them know that our ears are open, we also need to remember not to push them into revealing their biggest secret. It is for us to begin the conversation and let them know that we are available to talk when it suits them. But offer it properly, like a proposal to tackle a really tough puzzle together, not just a sympathetic, 'Ah bless you, I'm here if you need me.'

So, when faced with my tears, my dad did all he could do. He gave me a big hug. I didn't know what the hell was happening and I didn't know that it was something I could go to the doctors about. My mum did though. We were having dinner as a family one night and I got up before everyone had finished and started doing the washing up. Their conversations continued with a happy, easy-going tone to them, something I felt completely estranged from, and I felt it all come to a boil. I was overcome with a sudden rage of uncontrollable confusion and despair and I smashed a glass into the sink and cut my hand open. Mum got up, gave me a hug, said, 'Enough's enough' and took me to the doctor.

My mum only recently told me in detail about a breakdown of hers and diagnosis of clinical depression and anxiety. My first reaction was an aching pain in my heart for my younger mum. The second was a realisation that maybe this was why I ended up going down the same route – have I got my mum's brain? At the time, she was looking after three kids – eight, six and three years old – and didn't really have an understanding of depression and anxiety herself. It was not spoken about in those days. Having three kids, a modest house allowance and making sure all the washing, cleaning and dinners were all done every night of the week is more stressful than any normal nine-to-five job. Women all through history have not been given enough credit for what they do. They are the backbone of us all and any bloke who can't see that is just ignorant and has forgotten that they were once latched on to the boob of life, too. So why did my mum get to that point of despair? I believe it's because it wasn't spoken about, because she had to deal with all her stresses and anxieties alone. So much can be accomplished in an open and honest conversation. Through my mum telling me the story of her breakdown I began to understand the potential reasons for mine.

We were kids and playing, probably fighting. Mum asked us to stop quite a few times and when we didn't she slapped me around the face. I was eight. She said she took all her anger, confusion and stresses out on me, as I was the eldest. It was something she deeply regrets and felt instantly ashamed for. Being the little prick I was, I said that I was going to tell Dad. I can only imagine that being so unwell my mum thought that this small episode was the end of the world. She smashed the kitchen window and then attempted to get in the car. She said the car would have probably ended up in a ditch or through a brick wall. Thankfully my dad managed to stop her and put her to bed. The next day Mum took my sister Jenny to the doctor for a routine asthma check-up and, without my mum saying anything about the events the day before, the doctor told her that she had to come back in to talk about her mental health. The doc could sense that this was a woman on the edge of potential breakdown maybe suicide. He diagnosed mum with clinical depression and started her on a course of meds. She honestly believes that the doctor's observation that day saved her life. It's quite amazing that even twenty-four years ago it was really only doctors who could see it and friends and family couldn't. Back then there weren't any celebrities, icons or role models who spoke openly about their mental health. There still isn't enough of them now and I know they're out there. If the stats were the same in the nineties as they are now then one in four people had experience of depression and anxiety. That's one of the Spice Girls, three of Man United's starting line-up and one of these four male screen icons – John McClane (*Die Hard*), Martin Riggs (*Lethal Weapon*), Robocop and the Terminator. All four of them probably had mental health issues, to be fair – two of them constantly wore dirty white vests and the other two weren't sure whether they were robots or not.

I had no idea about any of this at the time, though, and neither did my poor parents. But it is thanks to that doctor that my mum knew what I needed to do to get help. On 20 October 2008 I filled out a form called HADS (Hospital Anxiety and Depression Scale). For a start, seeing the word 'Hospital' at the top of the page was pretty frightening – images of being tied up in some dungeon quickly formulated in my terrified, confused brain. Then my eyes quickly glanced down to the scoring table:

0–7 Normal
8–10 Borderline abnormal (borderline case)
11–21 Abnormal (case)

They may as well have slipped 'nut' in front of that 'case' because reading that I was a potential 'case' was worrying. My depression score was 13 and my anxiety 11. I was officially 'Abnormal'! Way to go on the damage limitation. The questions on this wonderful form all demanded an answer but never asked why. 'Do worrying thoughts go through your mind from time to time but not too often?' Take a pill. I think that if I had been prescribed a psychologist, rather than antidepressants, I may have never needed medication. It simply wasn't an option though. There wasn't a word about it from my doctor. I didn't even really know what psychotherapy was then. I trusted the doctor and did what she said. I went home that afternoon with a packet of citalopram – a SSRI (selective serotonin re-uptake inhibitor) – in my hand and no real comprehension of what a diagnosis of depression and acute anxiety actually meant. The dose was 20mg. Yes, doc, whatever you say, doc. I think I was too lazy or scared to research the answer and there didn't seem to be any in-depth explanation from her. I think all that happened was that I was given a handout to read. My damaged mental health was treated like a broken leg, in the sense that I had been sent to the doctors with a problem and now I had been given anti-depressants, so the problem had been dealt with. End of story. It's true that I needed the tablets as a short-term fix – a lift of serotonin to restart my engine and get me to a place where I could assess sanely what was happening to me and what I needed to do to change my life to prevent unhappiness. I know that now and my doctor should have known that then. But I was left to take the tablets for seven years without question. I also realise now that you can't selectively numb emotions; you can't say I don't want to feel sadness, loneliness, vulnerability but I'll have all the good stuff. When we numb, we numb everything – joy, purpose, real happiness. This happened to an extent when I took my meds but it also happens every day when people who aren't officially 'mentally unwell' use alcohol and drugs to suppress real emotions.

I took the tablets when I got home and hid the packet in between some books on my shelf – probably wedged between Richard Branson's autobiography and Richard Templar's *Rules of Life*, amongst many other success stories or self-help literature (bad ones chosen because of little research, although I did really like Branson's). I was immediately ashamed about the fact that I had to take a tablet to make me like everyone else. I didn't know anyone who was depressed, famous or otherwise, so from my point of view at the time, I was the only pathetic loser in the world who needed help putting on a smile. I remember my mum being pro-tablets and she was happy that I had them. I remember my dad questioning whether I actually needed them and trying to talk to me to solve it. He scratched his head as to what it might be that was making his son so upset. He'd always ask me, 'Are you sure you're not hiding anything from us?' I think he thought I was in trouble with drug dealers or I'd got someone pregnant, or perhaps I was gay and struggling to come out. He was convinced there was some sort of soap opera at play. There wasn't. But how could they understand? I hadn't told them that I'd been having suicidal thoughts so I don't think either of them really knew the extent of my problems. Dad was really good to have tried to talk to me to fix it and I made it difficult for him. I didn't feel that I could open up completely to either of them because of possible judgement. My dad was a hero to me. I had never been exposed to him being vulnerable or low or anything but a happy, mentally well dad. To admit to him that I couldn't follow in his footsteps was shameful to me.

The diagnosis and tablets made me worse initially. I was disappointed in myself. I felt ostracised. I was broken. With this self-pity came slight relief, though, too. I felt relieved that it wasn't just my problem now. I was happy that three other people knew my little-but-big secret. I thought maybe it would all be sorted now and I could pass on all responsibility to those guys and they would make it possible for me to go back to a life before all this sadness. I remember constantly thinking that no one wants to hear all this complaining and moaning and confusion. No one likes a glass-half-empty sort of person. 'Did you see that goal?' 'No, but have you thought about why we're all here?' It brings the mood down when everyone's trying to enjoy life. I had tried to enjoy life but the force of depression was too strong and it had swallowed me up.

After a few of weeks, though, I was back. I was playing football with a smile on my face again. I actually enjoyed having conversations with people. I was just so relieved not to be looking at the world in a negative way. It was almost addictive. I made sure that tiny pill went down my gullet as soon as I woke up in the morning. I felt positive. I felt worth in myself again. I was happy with who I was. I didn't hate myself.

CHAPTER FOUR

B: *SSRIs or selective serotonin reuptake inhibitors are a type of antidepressant tablet for people with clinical depression. Now, they are very effective, used by millions across the world BUT they also have some pretty major side effects. Side effects Tim had been labouring under for quite some time.*

I was on tablets now and it was time to jump back on the treadmill of my life. I think they took around six weeks to kick in properly but I felt like I was in control of my destiny again. I had taken back the reins from the dark devil headfuck who had been driving me into a pit of life-long sadness. I started to sleep a little better than I had for a long time and I think that made a huge difference to my motivation to live happily. I had the energy to get up and get out the house and go to football training or go out on a Friday night to see mates or even clean the kitchen floor for my mum. She asked me to do it a million times when I felt depressed and I wanted to rig that floor up with dynamite and light it with me in the middle as some sort of final stand against the Grayburn regime of child slavery. Having the energy to get up and work and do things meant that I didn't have time to sit and wallow and think about how much I was disappointed in myself or how much of a bad place the world was. The medication gave me the encouragement I needed to do something actively about it; I mean, I wasn't delivering aid to Iraq or anything, but I also wasn't lying in bed at two in the afternoon trying to fix it all with a philosophical equation.

I started to notice that I had patience with people again and that made me happy because I was communicating with humans and not shutting myself away as much. Before taking the tablets I just wanted to be alone but, at the same time, I never wanted to be alone. I didn't like to be around people because I felt as if they could see what was happening to me and I didn't want to admit it to them. Arrogantly, I also felt that most human beings were idiots and I couldn't understand how they could be happy when everything was so terrible. I was consumed by my own misery. Once I was alone I felt like the loneliest person in the world, though, and wished I could just be sitting with people but with no one saying anything. If only I could have spoken about it to friends and family we would have all been on the same page. But when you're depressed, though, you constantly have conflicting thoughts like that – you want to be with people but you don't. You want to talk but you don't. You want to go for a run but you don't. You want to die but you don't. You get the picture. The tablets took over as a kind of personal consultant for my everyday choices. More often than not they encouraged me towards the positive choice of getting out there and being a member of society. Physically I started to look healthier, too, and my face wasn't so drawn. The dark circles under my eyes went and my appetite came back. It wasn't a miracle tablet that changed everything in an instant but over time it built me back up from the ground.

In terms of side effects I remember having a dry mouth constantly, manageable headaches and an increase of weird dreams (I say increase because I've always been a weird dreamer; every morning of my life I wake up thinking, 'You're weird, mate!'). I was very agitated and pretty itchy all the time but, apart from that, I was OK. Those were the initial side effects and, as time went on over the years, more started to creep in. I don't know whether that was because of adjusting doses or whether, as my body didn't need them as much, the positive effects of the medication turned negative. I don't know. Either way the side effects at the beginning were all manageable and I was just grateful for the positive effects – they outweighed the negative and that was all that mattered.

I got a job in a pub and met a girl called Maddy, who

I quickly became fascinated with. We went out on a few dates and then got together. She was five years younger than me and was probably just what I needed – an excuse to rewind time and act twenty years old again. She was fun, creative and carefree. She had her own mental illness story, which she and her mum had told me about. Not knowing about mine, Maddy was not so keen on revealing all but she did none the less. She was bullied at school for being overweight – she was a chubby, pretty funny-looking, but adorable kid – and she then developed an eating disorder that made her really ill. Fucking bullies – you should be ashamed of yourselves! Anyway, good prevailed over evil and she battled and beat her eating disorder. She also grew into a tall, blonde, beautiful woman. She was spotted and became a really successful model featuring in *Vogue* and all sorts of ad campaigns. Her mental illness story was a quick and successful one, so perhaps that's why they were more at ease about disclosing it. I wasn't. I was right at the beginning of my story and I didn't know whether there would be success at the end of it or not. At the time the stigma surrounding depression and anxiety trumped the stigma surrounding eating disorders. Perhaps that is because you can see an obvious physical change when you are suffering from an eating disorder. Isn't that strange? You don't have to be a scientist to figure out that bulimia and anorexia are mental issues that lead to physical ones. If depressives actually turned blue, would that remove the taboo? Do we need to see people's suffering with our own eyes, rather that just having to believe them when they tell us what is happening on the inside? At the time there were no social media campaigns or news articles or even widely known mental health charities. For me, there was just the diagnosis of depression and anxiety, only known by me, my GP and my parents. I was no way near ready to tell my girlfriend, or anyone else for that matter.

On paper I was lucky – I had a girlfriend, I kept fit, I partied and travelled a lot, had no real responsibilities and I had good friends. I loved life and I didn't want to ruin one minute of it by telling everyone my secret. I worried that they would all call me a fake. The taboo had me by the balls. And I felt comfortable with that – I didn't want to talk about it plain and simple. The only time I was reminded of what was wrong with me was when I pushed those books aside to get a tablet. I swallowed it, put the packet back and pushed the books together again, just like I was shutting the gateway into that real, sad hopeless world.

A year passed on the tablets and I was happy. I was a glass-half-full sort of person now and I had learnt to forget about my problems. I moved out of home again but this time I moved in with Nick. I quit my job in the pub and got a job in a call centre because it was better money. I hated it so much, though, that even the tablets couldn't stop me from dipping back into depression. The mundane nature of the job gave me no choice but to confront my problems. It gave me a reason to think about who I was and what my purpose in life was. After just a couple of weeks the symptoms came back. I wasn't sleeping again and I was sad and felt hopeless. I was so negative about things and I couldn't break my life down into manageable chunks. I couldn't look at the job as a stepping stone on the way to bigger and better things, or use my time to discover what it was I really wanted to do. For me, that was it – my entire future: working in a job I hated and renting a room, living with a couple. I searched for a different route but just couldn't come up with one. I didn't know what I wanted to do for a career. It felt like the harder I tried, the more I pushed myself into depression. I remember annoying some poor bloke on the phone trying to sell him something he didn't want and in my sales writing pad I drew a picture of the grim reaper holding a sign with my initials on it. I didn't think anything of it; I didn't see that this was a sign that things weren't right. It was like my brain was sending me a signal through a sketch and I was the blind artist. A few days later I drew a woman giving birth and the baby was crawling into a giant apple. Written on the apple were words such as school, family, hate, love, work, pain and all sorts of human emotions and usual life events. At the top of the apple was a worm coming out of it with angel wings. Pretty weird, huh? I think I was telling myself that life was all those things and then we just get buried and turn into worms. Pretty dark but my niggling questions about the purpose of life were obviously back, too. Thankfully I did see this as a warning sign and I took myself back to the doctor. She upped my dose to 40mg and said, 'Let's see how you get on with that.' I didn't talk to my parents about this little relapse and I don't know why. I checked in with them every now and then, but I had been so happy since I started the medication, that they both must of thought that I was all good and that I was just getting on with life.

Maddy and I weren't going so well, though, either. I don't know whether my dip back into depression had anything to do with it. It was probably one of a few things. She had decided to put her modelling aside and go to uni in Leeds to discover herself as a 21-year-old artist, so we were struggling with a long-distance relationship and that was undoubtedly a big factor. We were in completely different stages of our lives – she was young and eager to meet new people and party and figure her own shit out. I had gone through that already. Still, we stayed together but it was coming apart at the seams. The higher dose worked temporarily in heightening my mood but I do remember feeling a big increase in the side effects – mainly the drowsiness, headaches and agitation. But the side effects were pretty similar to the symptoms of depression, so it was hard to decipher which was which. It wasn't a good balance for me but it did keep me from thinking about life and death for the time being and that's what was most important.

I started looking for work in London to get out of the bubble I'd found myself in and to get in the mix, to try and feel enjoyment again. I looked hopelessly on websites trying to get some inspiration but nothing stood out. I signed up to most of the recruitment firms but nothing they sent was interesting. One woman called me and said she'd got me an interview at the BBC – they had seen my CV and had asked me to come in to interview for a job as a researcher. I thought that sounded all right so I dragged myself all the way from Oxford to White City. The job turned out to be nothing like the one that had been explained to me by the recruitment lady and the woman interviewing me basically shouted at me for wasting her time. I shouted back at her and said, 'You asked me to come in for an interview. Don't shout at me! Stick your job right up your bbbb. . . butt hole, ya bitch.' I was so angry and, even though it wasn't my fault, that woman made me feel like the biggest piece of shit in the world and I remember crying on my way home. Not crying because I hadn't got the job, it was a real hopeless cry.

I kept looking for work and nothing came up. Weeks went by until one day an old colleague from when I had worked in media in Oxford called and said there was a job going at a new agency in Holborn. She sorted me an interview. Sitting on the train down to London heading for Maxus, the media agency, I remember looking out of the window trying to hold back the tears at the thought of my uselessness. I had no self-esteem whatsoever and I just couldn't seem to stop myself from wanting to cry. I had got to the point where I didn't even know why I wanted to cry. It was just there. I was suffocated by emotion. I knew I wasn't going to be good enough to get the job. I told myself that I was too dumb and I'd just embarrass myself pretending to be the man for the job. The self-doubt and worthlessness – both symptoms of depression – were out in full force. I got home feeling defeated before I even knew the outcome. But two days later I got an email saying I'd got the job. In that one instant I felt like my life was about to turn around. I had actually been impressive enough to secure a job in a top media agency in London! I found out later that I'd only got the job because they'd heard I was a lot of fun and that my formal interview performance was appalling. Who cares? What mattered at the time was that I felt like I was good enough. My confidence was back to a degree. I'd been given a boost and I was itching to get involved and experience all that London had to offer.

I was 26 and in the best city in the world. I was a village boy dumped right in the middle of the action. My boss at the time and friend John, a real cockney, does a hilarious impression of what he thinks I looked like on the first day of the job: wide-eyed bumpkin with a backpack scanning the high-rise buildings and hustle and bustle of the city. I was meeting new people every day and being taken out to the nicest restaurants, bars and clubs the city had to offer. I was having the time of my life and no one needed to know I was taking tablets to curb my depression and anxiety issues.

My relationship with Maddy completely fell apart. That was the last bit of my past to go before I really could start again. I had repackaged myself – Tim Grayburn, the fun, single, free, young man who was here for a good time. London was the biggest playground I'd ever seen. Every day was so different from the last and it was like I was being taken through the days by a stampede of wild drunken horses that I had no choice but to just go with it. I dived right in. I had been travelling so wasn't completely naive but the beautiful diversity of London and living right in the middle of it made me feel alive again. I wanted a taste of everything.

I started off living in Clapham with a mate from home called Sam. We were both on shit salaries and were new to London so we didn't know the geography of the city or how it worked. But it was a lot of fun figuring it all out. The flat came up through someone he knew and, much like finding a university by just moving to Chichester without knowing the place, I did the same with Clapham. I remember having so little money that I used to nick my dinners every night from the supermarkets like a right scallywag. Meanwhile, I was taking my tablets every day and even Sam didn't know. I felt so far from depressed that I really never thought about it. My pills were labelled by the day and I would often find myself missing four or five days at a time with no real problems. I thought to myself that I had been fixed, that my depression was a thing of the past and that it must have been situational; it must have been part of that time in my life when I was lost. I was in London with a career and I felt like a normal person. Was I now just taking the tablets out of habit and security? Could I live without them and would I live more comfortably without the side effects? I decided it was time to jack the tablets in. There was nothing wrong with me, I was sure of it. I wanted to see if somehow my brain had been fixed and had returned to how it used to feel.

So, I just stopped taking the tablets, cold turkey. I was having such a good time I wasn't even monitoring my mental health as I came off them. Roughly two weeks after deciding to give them up, I woke up and, as soon as I opened my eyes, I could feel it. The ringing in my ears like an alarm clock had woken up my sleeping Anxiety Giant. It felt like someone was watching me when I lay in bed, when I was in the shower and all the way into work. I wasn't sad but I was petrified at how little control I felt that I had over myself. I remember calling Dad at lunchtime and asking him what to do. I think he suggested that I go home and sleep it off but, like an idiot, I didn't listen to him. I didn't want to let anyone down at work. I didn't present with any physical symptoms so I didn't want to be called a skiver. What I needed, I thought, were those tablets back in my system as soon as possible. I got back home that night and frantically searched for them in my room like I was gasping for oxygen. It took me a couple of weeks to balance myself out again but, when I felt I was back in the driving seat, I made the decision to never ever try that again.

The lease on the Clapham flat was up and Sam had got a job back in Oxford so he moved out. It was hard for him because he'd moved down without a job in place so he had been temping for most of the six months and never really got settled. I had a good summer in Clapham but I wanted to be in East London. I was continuously drawn to the place. The rawness and diversity was what I loved about it; there was always something going on. I had to move there. I met a girl called Ali, who was a friend of Stav's girlfriend Emily. We hit it off straight away; she had just come out of a relationship with someone who sounded like a right bell and who wasn't very nice to her. She was a sweet, attractive, bright, big-hearted girl, who was also a little bit nuts; just what I was after at the time. She met a guy in Ibiza called "Jon boy" who told her that he'd just bought a flat right at the top of the Hackney Road and he was looking for a room-mate. She introduced us and it was a match made in heaven. We were both new to the area and we were both immature dickheads. It was perfect.

I was really happy and didn't feel depressed but I had not enjoyed my mini anxiety meltdown. I had to find a balance. At the time I didn't know that it was anxiety that I was suffering from. I didn't know what was wrong with me but I was sure it was something other than 'depression'. I remembered that I was in a good place during the year I was on 20mg and so I thought that maybe I needed to go back to that dose. I arranged to go back to the doctor's, which was literally next door to my new flat. I told them that I wanted to go back on to the 20mg dose and they agreed that it was a good idea. I don't remember ever explaining what happened to me when I came off the meds cold turkey. I don't think I could find the words to articulate the anxiety attacks I was experiencing or the lower level anxiety I was experiencing most days. I'm pretty certain there wasn't much effort on the part of the doctor to dig deeper either. I think he knew exactly what was wrong with me but didn't have the time to explain it in layman's terms and just saw me as another person who'll just trust what the doctor says. And I was. After a few weeks on the new dose, my perfect balance returned again and I continued to live my life as I had before. I took a tablet every day, like a sort of ritual in that parallel universe of divided books, and then returned to the real world where everything was fine and I was normal just like everyone else.

I didn't talk to Ali about my depression. Thinking back now, she would have completely understood if I had sat down and spoken to her about it. But I didn't. I didn't want her to think that I was a pussy. I thought she was with me because I was confident and had my shit together. I didn't want to risk ruining her opinion of me. It turns out she kind of knew anyway. We were close and in a tight relationship, so it makes sense that she had realised that something was not quite right. Maybe she also knew that I didn't want to talk about it so she didn't bring it up either. Besides, I was happy and rarely showed signs of being someone who was clinically depressed. It just broke through every now and then to remind me that it was still there and that we still had unfinished business. Maybe on one of those episodes she saw that something was wrong and put two and two together. Either way, I regret not opening up. A family member of Ali's also suffered from depression and she was great with them; she was perfectly empathetic and I saw first hand how caring she was. And yet I still couldn't open up about myself. Maybe she was a guardian sent to me to help but I wasn't quite ready to accept it. For a number of reasons we eventually split and I was safe again from the possibility of having to reveal my secret life to anyone.

I was now twenty-nine years old and my childhood idea of being settled with kids by the time I was thirty was officially unachievable. I wasn't bothered, though, because I had known for a long time that I had too much to see and do before I entered that world. I think a lot of people my age grew up with a pressure to be settled with a family by the time they were thirty. I don't know why. I guess our biological clocks were always ticking in the background, but you should only have children and settle when you want to, not because you've read somewhere that you need to. I wanted to but I wasn't going to pressure myself into it. It just started to be something I thought about. I knew I wanted children in the future and that it would probably happen in my thirties, but I was going to see my twenties out first and enjoy myself. Work was going well and my mental health was pretty stable. That year became the biggest party year. I felt that I had to squeeze in as much as I could. I completely neglected my depression and anxiety and lived like I didn't give a shit about anything. And I didn't. Looking back now, for a large part of that year I wasn't actually happy at all, but I distracted myself enough so that I didn't have to think about it. I was out drinking and messing about so much that I looked like I was really happy. That kind of stuff was happiness for me at that point in my life; I wasn't thinking clearly enough to know what true happiness was. I don't think I'd ever experienced it. I'm not even sure you can define it.

By the end of the year cracks were starting to show and the depression and anxiety were starting to pour out of them. I was struggling with balancing the pressures of work and keeping up my lifestyle of late nights and drinking heavily. Things started going wrong all the time. I was getting into trouble at work for turning up late and being drunk. I was annoying my housemate by being loud and drunk. I was being unfair to girls I was seeing and I also got arrested for having a fight in a bar. Some lads started on me and we had a fight and then they pressed charges, even though they had started it. I couldn't believe it; it was self-defence. I just remember that I was having fun and minding my own business and then two guys cornered me and said they were going to do me in. I ended up being arrested three days later in front of my boss and had to wait six months to go to court to face charges of GBH, which were then dropped to ABH. If I was guilty, I would most probably lose my job and then I'd be in a real mess. It summed up my life at that point; I was so unstable with no direction and I was destructive and angry. I couldn't even take my medication responsibly. I'd run out or lose the tablets and then I'd have to try and arrange an emergency appointment to get another prescription from the doctor. I made up all sorts of excuses with work to get to those appointments. The only ones available were always during working hours, which was ridiculous because I was so busy I felt like I couldn't ask to leave the office for an hour and half to get across to East London, have an appointment and then get back without a good enough reason. My fault of course for being so disorganised but still. At the time I believed that being on the verge of a breakdown wasn't a good enough reason to go to the doctor, so I'd make all sorts of stuff up. One day I managed to get an appointment at 6pm, which was technically out of office hours but, in reality, I would usually still have been working away then. Every time I went, I had a different GP (it wasn't the best surgery), which wasn't great for someone who feels vulnerable talking about their illness. But, in all honesty, I was getting to the point where I didn't care any more. I didn't really care about anything. At that 6pm appointment, though, I ended up talking to a lovely woman who really tried to speak to me about how I felt and what I should do to try and feel as normal as possible. I said that I wanted to come off the tablets because I was convinced it was the side effects that were making me feel ill. I told her about my previous attempt to come off and she suggested I wean myself off over a period of time: about six weeks. We put a plan in place and she said that she would call me to check my progress every two weeks. She never called. I tried to call her but I wasn't allowed to be put through on the phone and the only time I could get an appointment with her was some time in the working day in two-to-three weeks' time. After two weeks of weaning myself off, I started to feel wobbly and my anxiety was becoming a problem at work. I was still drinking a lot and not really focusing on getting myself better, so I quit the weaning and carried on taking the tablets to make life easier. I didn't feel like I had enough support around me to come off them properly. I remember struggling to keep up the act of someone who wasn't suffering. I came out of the doctor's one day and, just as I was walking down the steps, my flatmate walked past and said, 'What's up with you, then?' I felt like I'd been caught with my hand in the antidepressant cookie jar. I came up with an elaborate lie about a problem with my liver and I had to go in to have some checks. I thought this was a good lie to stick to since it meant I could use it for a while any time I had to go back in to get a prescription. Isn't it sad that I couldn't bring myself to tell him that I had an appointment to discuss treatment for my chemical unbalance, or whatever the fuck was going on in my head? And that a liver problem would be preferable to a mental health problem. I think part of the issue was that I didn't know how to explain what was wrong with me. Four years had passed since I had been diagnosed and I still had no idea what the real cause or reason was for me being clinically depressed. I still don't, even as I write a book about it!

I was halfway through being twenty-nine and figured it was time to move on in life. I wanted to settle down. I decided to move out of East London and live on my own. I moved into a one-bed flat in Elephant and Castle. I hadn't really thought it through – I was miserable and so tucking myself away on my own in an area I wasn't familiar with was not a good idea but, at the time, I thought it was. I was seeing someone and she came over every now and then but it wasn't anything serious. I had never let anyone close enough to see my problems – not because I didn't think anyone was good enough to know what was going on, but because I was ashamed. This time, though, I thought maybe I should talk to her about it before it got serious. The way I saw it, if I didn't say anything then I'd be stuck in the same situation I was with Maddy and Ali, where I was in love and felt too ashamed to reveal everything. I had hidden it for four years now but it was breaking through, leaking out like an over-stuffed salad box. The lifestyle I had enjoyed in London for the past three years had run its course of distracting me from what was going on in my head. So, I finally decided to talk to someone about it. She seemed to be cool and non-judgemental so she was the obvious choice. Plus, if she decided that she didn't want to stick around, then not a huge amount of love would be lost. It was just another weekend; we arranged to meet up at the Southbank and go for some lunch somewhere. We were strolling along and I said, 'I want to tell you something.' She said, 'OK, what's up?' And then I told her. I just did it. Fucking hell, here I go, I'm letting out my biggest secret, one I'm incredibly ashamed of, and one that, I think, makes me a pussy, unmasculine, unattractive and pathetic. I told her that I was struggling with depression and my anxiety was really picking up pace – it was starting to affect my work and my daily living. Two or three days later the relationship was over. For reasons of her own, she wasn't sticking around for a nutcase.

I moved out of the flat straight away and retreated back to Bethnal Green so I could turn myself back into the carefree bloke who goes out all the time and sleeps around. It was fun and a welcome distraction, but it wasn't what I really wanted. I wanted to open up. It was going to take something or someone pretty special to make me talk about it again.

CHAPTER FIVE

B: *Hello. I'm Bryony Kimmings. I'm a loud-mouth, feminist performance artist from London. If you aren't familiar with my artwork, you can usually find me sniffing around some kind of social stigma or trying to tear down a terrible taboo. And I often work with people who don't usually grace the stage.*

I met Bryony the night after I got back from a work trip to Portugal. It was exactly one week after my thirtieth birthday and the seven days of celebrating were supposed to have ended that day. My old friend Toby convinced me to join him at a pop-up bar, though, when all I wanted to do was go home and sleep. I got a shot of adrenalin as soon as I walked in and laid my eyes on her. I was suddenly more awake than I had ever been. Everything around her was blurred and insignificant. It was like a private viewing in my head of one of those corny

Hollywood moments when everything slows down and there's just a spotlight on this beautiful creature who is dancing as if she were in her bedroom all alone. Granted that meant she was dancing like a maniac and rubbing her tits up and down and pretending to kick strangers in the balls, but it was beautiful to me. I was intrigued; she was the one person in that room who was nothing like the others. I fancied her from the off – but I wasn't her type, apparently, and she didn't fancy me straight away. Defiant, I cornered her like I was trying to catch a loose chicken. We smoked a cigarette together and I didn't say much. I watched as she bounced off the people around her, full of energy with a 'I don't give a fuckness' about her that had me hooked. As the night went on, I decided that I wasn't going to sit and wait for some other bloke to snatch her away from me. I went in for the kiss; she tilted her head back and said something like, 'Whoa there, freckles, I'm not that easy.' Damn it. Maybe I was too tired, after all. I was losing her. I didn't want to give up. Toby and I managed to get ourselves invited back to a party at her friend Daisy's house and Bryony and I ended up having a night of good ol' sex. Four times in six hours; we couldn't get enough of each other. It turned out Toby was doing the same thing in the next bedroom with Daisy. We all hung out together the next day and had a day of laughs and free loving.

After a few days of spending every minute together, it was apparent to me that this wasn't just any other girl.

She was special. She was so unique that it sparked an excitement in me every day and made me realise how bored I was with living a normal life. She gave me energy and we couldn't keep our hands off each other. We laughed from the moment we woke until we went to sleep. It was a summer I'll never forget. We mainly just rolled around in the park and went on little holidays. It was a time of discovery, drunken stupidity, and a feeling that life had really arrived. We indulged in one another while the rest of the world continued around us. We were so comfortable with each other that we could almost read one another's mind. We lay on the bed one evening and just looked at each other and I said, 'You love me, don't you?' I was shocked at my arrogance. Where did that come from? I would never have dreamed of being that confident before, but I just knew that she was feeling exactly the same way as I did so I had to confirm it. We went out to celebrate, after having sex, of course. We decided that I should move in with her, even though it had only been a couple of months. I was living in a dream every day, bouncing up like I was ten years younger every morning and ready to go into work. The problem was, though, I didn't actually want to go to work and leave her lying in bed. Bryony's an artist who decides her own time; she isn't an animal who can be contained in an office environment for ten hours a day. At the time she was working on a theatre show she was making with her sweetheart eight-year-old niece called *Credible*

Likeable Superstar Role Model: a classic Bryony title, not the 'norm'. It was about the sexualisation of children in the media and she had something to say about it. That was another reason why I was hooked – I had found someone who was just as pissed off about shit things in the world as I was. The difference was that she was doing something about it. And doing it well.

Each day was the same for me: get up; go to work with a post-sex smile on my face; get through as much of the day as possible without thinking about Bryony; get home; go to the park for dinner; go for some drinks; go home and have sex until we fall asleep. Perfect. Nothing could stop us. Or so I thought. There was just one little thing that was bothering me. I had met this person and she seemed to have her cards on the table – did I really have mine on there, too? I didn't want to mess things up by telling her my little secret. I had a feeling that she would understand but there was no way I was going to risk ruining everything by telling her about my depression – especially after what happened when I told my last girlfriend. I decided that I was in too deep to reveal anything. I liked her too much to risk telling her and having her not understand.

I didn't feel depressed but the side effects of the tablets were starting to bother me. I made my mind up that I was going to wean myself off them again. This time, however, I was going to make a few adjustments to my previous weaning plan. I was going to stop drinking as much and try to quit smoking all together. Smoking stimulates the release of dopamine in the brain and dopamine helps us trigger positive feelings. People with depression are believed to have low levels of dopamine or problems triggering it. Even though in the short run smoking encourages the release of dopamine, in fact it encourages the brain to switch off its own dopamine-making mechanism so, in the long run, the supply to your brain decreases. I started to understand that if I was going to do this properly and try and figure out exactly what it was that makes me depressed, I needed to get back to my organic self slowly. I needed to cut out all the mind-altering substances I was taking, like nicotine, caffeine and alcohol for a start. Once I had managed to do that, I could come off the antidepressants and really see if I needed them or not. It was a pretty logical plan. The problem was it meant life was just about to get very boring compared to the life I was used to. We were still only three months into our relationship and we had had three months of nothing but nicotine, caffeine and alcohol. What would it do to our relationship if I stopped it all with no explanation? Thankfully, Bryony was starting to think we were both drinking too much and she wanted to settle down a bit and have a detox. Perfect. We could do it together, without her knowing my reasons why. I thought that if I came off the tablets slowly and was responsible about it, then I had a chance of doing it on my own without having to tell my girlfriend or needing the support of a doctor, who would probably never call back anyway. I might not have been ready to tell Bryony about what was going on, but I was happy that I had her in my corner. I decided I was going to beat it on my own. I hoped I'd be fine and then it could just be a secret I could bury along with all the empty pill packets.

PART II

CHAPTER ONE

11th September 2013 at 13:17

Oh gosh Tim,

I have got myself into a right tizz, darling. I know it's a busy day for you so ignore my text. I thought it better to send an email anyway.

I grabbed your black backpack to pop my laptop in to take into town; I wanted to balance out my back as it's twingey.

I emptied it as it just looked like gym stuff, I thought you wouldn't mind, but in it I found some citalopram.

I didn't know you took them?! Did I?

I am racking my brains to figure out if this is something HUGE that I did know, but I am not finding the information anywhere. I know there was talk of some time a while ago where you did have a spell of depression when you were living at home, I thought, I think that was a very brief conversation right in the early days, but I was very shocked when I found them. I had to sit down on the edge of the bed.

I want to talk to you about it and now you are out for the evening and I am trapped without a fucking phone with a hideous hangover and I feel like you have kept something big from me and I am wondering why, seeing as we are so close to one another. Or I think we are. I am sorry if that seems awfully dramatic, but I can't put these two pieces of information together: my lovely, open, happy, sexually ferocious Tim and these drugs that I have seen turn my nearest into zombies.

Please explain to me. I am all ears. I am all heart. I am all here. But I am confused.

I can call you later from the theatre, I am free all afternoon as just in a session with Nina. If that is any good. If not tonight or tomorrow.

Am I being a twat?!

Love you

Bry xxxx

Ah. Secret is out. I got back to my desk after lunch that day and read that email twenty times. My heart stopped and I went into damage limitation mode. Can I lie about it? Not likely. I'm going to have to tell her the truth and then pack my bags as she wipes her brow saying to herself, 'Phew, I've avoided a mental case.' Talk about a roller coaster, one minute I was at the very highest peak, touching the clouds, and the next instant I'm down at the bottom, off the rails and already in the scrap heap. I hated my depression in that moment; it was fucking things up for me again. I was feeling happy but it couldn't let me have it. It put its twatty walking stick around my neck and pulled me right back in under its wing. I texted her and said that I'd explain later.

I walked home to Clapton from Holborn very slowly that evening to avoid the confession for as long as I could. I thought about the email over and over again. It was typically dramatic of Bryony – was it 'HUGE'? At the time, I thought so. Looking at it now, not at all. I thought it was ironic that she had finished the email with, 'I can call you from the theatre.' I felt like the email was part of theatre – the theatre of my hidden life. It was now out of my hands and all I had to do was tell the truth and wait to see what her reaction would be. After all, she'd asked me to explain and she'd said that she was there for me. And I loved her for that; I kind of felt safe. I put the key in the front door and turned it clockwise at the pace of a second hand on a grandfather clock. I walked into the kitchen and she gave me a big hug and made a cup of tea. We sat down on the bed and we talked all through the night. I reassured her that I wouldn't keep secrets from her in the future and that my problems lay with my past not the present. I also explained that the tablets didn't turn me into a zombie and that they had been great for me but I believed that I didn't need them any more. This was the first time I had ever heard of anyone talking about antidepressants on a personal level, other than my parents and the GPs. I explained that the withdrawal from them was tough and that I would need her help. It felt good to hear that she knew people close to her who had also been on medication and had suffered from depression and/or anxiety. It was nice to hear but they were both women and I still felt ashamed and emasculated. Even in 2013, it was so much more of a taboo than it is now. At the time, I hadn't heard any of the statistics that circulate in the news and on social media regarding mental illness. I didn't know that it affected so many of us. I didn't know there were other blokes who had the same thing and took the same medication. I never felt like I was part of a tribe. She reassured me that she didn't think anything less of me and that she wasn't going anywhere. She understood. We celebrated with sex and then went to sleep.

As the days went by, Bryony got used to the idea that I wasn't the perfectly rounded stud she thought she'd met. She says the revelation made her love me even more because she had worried that I was too rounded, boring, with nothing complicated about me. It gave her inquisitive mind something to work with. I mentioned to her again that, even though I was on the tablets and felt great, I really thought that I didn't need them any more. I believed I would feel just as great without them. I told her about my previous stupid attempt to come off them and we came up with a plan much the same as the one I had already considered – no drink, no drugs, no smoking, lots of exercise and healthy eating, along with weaning myself off the meds over a period of three months. If all went well I would be med free in time to enjoy Christmas and start 2014 off with a clear consciousness of happiness. I went back to the doctor and told them. We agreed on the plan – I was to take 20mg for one month, 10mg for the second and 5mg for the third.

I was doing OK. I was definitely feeling wobbly but I put that down to the drastic change of lifestyle and rebalancing of chemicals in my brain. I was going to the gym five days a week, I had completely quit caffeine, I was drinking once maybe twice a week rather than four or five nights a week and my diet was like a pro-cross champions. I also started to have acupuncture and I found that it really helped me deal with the stress of the withdrawal symptoms, emotionally and physically. It helped with my anxiety, in particular; it calmed me. I slept throughout the first two sessions, which I was amazed at because I very rarely slept if I wasn't drunk or in my bed in pitch darkness and peaceful quietness.

As the twelfth week of the plan drew closer, though,

I started to get very wobbly – I couldn't think straight, I had severe headaches, I was tearful, physically sick and I felt like I was losing my grip on reality a little. I felt like this for a good three weeks but went into work every day and hid behind a fake smile, putting even more pressure on my broken self. It was becoming hard to hide how I was feeling. Friends at work were asking me how I was in that way with a raised eyebrow, 'Arrrrre you all right?' 'NO I'M NOT FUCKING ALL RIGHT! MY BRAIN IS SPLILLING OUT OF MY EARS, MATE' is what I desperately wanted to say but, of course, I replied with, 'Yeah, I'm fine' and got back to dying inside. When it comes to mental illness, the person who's concerned has no choice but to take your word for it, if you say you are OK; they can't see what state your brain is actually in. It's not like there's a bone sticking through your chest so that they are able to insist that you're not really all right. 'Ah well, he must be stressed' was usually the conclusion.

I needed to come up with something to monitor my progress or, rather, my regression, as it was panning out. I decided to keep a diary to keep track on how I felt. I made a new note in my iPhone and called it 'D Diary'.

D Diary

9th November – Started feeling depressed, can't find excitement in anything

13th November – *Feel better today, not as blue*
14th November – *Not blue but tired and feel sick,
      finding it hard to concentrate*
7th December – *Last tablet*
8th December – *Feel pretty down*
9th December – *Feel very shaky and emotional, phys-
      ically sick*

I was watching the clock at work from around 11am, desperate for home time, which seemed like years away. I just had to get through the day. I decided to hide in the toilets, thinking that if I could just leave the office and go on a long walk, breathing slowly, I would regain some sense of saneness. That was all I needed to do, I thought over and over again. As soon as it hit 17:30 I was up and out. I never usually left on time so it raised a few suspicions. I was so focused on leaving the office that when I got out on to the pavement I froze. I didn't know how I was going to get back home; I may as well have fallen into a teleport trap and landed in the middle of Tokyo. A trip I took everyday suddenly seemed impossible to me for some reason. I gave it a go, though. I got on a bus on the wrong side of the road and started to head in the wrong direction. I realised what a stupid mistake I'd made, so I got off at the next stop and decided to walk instead. My mind was so occupied with how I felt that it didn't have the resources to do everyday tasks. I got a mile or so into the walk home and went into an off licence to buy some cigarettes. I ripped open the packet and lit one, hoping that it would stimulate whatever dopamine I might have left in my brain. I walked across the road without looking at the oncoming traffic and was centimetres away from being hit by a car. I felt like an alien with all these cars coming at me, beeping their horns and shouting out the window, 'Oi, you twat, get out of the road!' I'm losing it, I thought. Must get home. I stood on the other side of the road, having escaped some sort of real life Space Invader game, and I realised that I'd lost my bag. Panic kicked in. It had my wallet in it, my keys and, most importantly at the time, my fags. I crossed the road to go back into the shop and almost got hit by a bus this time around. That's when I really started to worry about my safety. I called Bryony but got no answer. I called my dad and cried down the phone to him, telling him that I didn't know what was happening to me and that I was fucked up. I can't really remember what he said but the poor, old sod must have been terrified and felt so helpless. I got my bag from the shop, sat on a bench and closed my eyes, begging for some clarity. After a few minutes I stood up, composed myself and started to walk home. I must have been walking at the pace of a baby's crawl but in my head it felt like I was Usain Bolt. Everything was exaggerated – every sound, light, movement – much like when I crashed my car. I was having a severe anxiety meltdown.

The weaning plan had quite clearly not worked. I had

done so well and stuck by the rules – apart from the drinking and smoking, which lasted two weeks but wasn't nearly as heavy as it was before. I got through the door and Bryony took one look at me and took me into the bedroom to lie down on the bed. I cried and told her that I was broken. She cuddled me and in the peace of that room I slowly started to get back to normality. I was still trembling but could almost speak and think clearly again. I told Bryony that I just needed a good night's sleep and I'd be fine to go into work in the morning. She was having none of it. She said that it was time I let work know that the months of pretending was making me even more ill and it had to stop now before something bad happened. We disagreed on it for hours until I finally conceded.

10th December 2013 at 23:24

Boys,

Five years ago I was diagnosed with clinical depression and was put on antidepressants and have been on them ever since. I haven't told you this before because I felt embarrassed and felt like, in the most part, I had it under control.

I attempted to come off the tablets a few years ago and failed so just reverted back to taking them. I didn't realise at the time that it's incredibly hard to come off the drugs and cope with normal day life as the chemicals in my brain rebalance.

As you know, I've had a few lifestyle changes recently – laying off the drink and generally looking after myself. This is because I decided 3 months ago that I wanted to come off them properly, with the support of my doctor and Bryony, because I felt like I was better.

I've been weaning myself off citalopram for 3 months. My last tablet was this Saturday just gone. Since then I've felt the full effects of the withdrawal – anxiety, fogginess, sickness, tearfulness, confusion of the slightest matters.

As you can imagine, me not mentioning this for so long being a good example, this is very hard for me to spill on a personal and professional level. I hate to let you both down, I feel weak and ashamed, especially when I know how busy we are, but I cannot come in tomorrow. I need to see the doctor as soon as possible.

This isn't permanent and I do think I will get better but it might take some time. I need you to bear with me while I get help from the doctors. I'll let you know what the doctor says tomorrow. I know I don't need to ask but can you keep this between yourselves and advise me on how to let Kirsten formally know my situation once I've seen the doctor.

Cheers,
Tim

Now four people, other than my parents and doctor, knew the depth of my secret – Bryony, my ex who did a runner, and John and Rod, my bosses. The boys were great and both of them replied with a promise of complete discretion and understanding. I still felt so ashamed, though. Would I ever get promoted? Surely they'd think I was completely incapable of doing my job? These were all the sorts of worries I had now that I had revealed my illness. But I also felt a smidgen of weight disappear from my shoulders; a flickering of relief. I wanted to unload more but I didn't know how and I was scared to. John and Rod let me know that I could take my time but all three of us knew we had a big deadline creeping up and I was needed. I went back to work after just a couple of days, which was far too soon and Bryony was furious about it. I should have listened to her.

So I was back in work and just pretending I was well. I still hadn't truly confronted my problem. There was one difference, however; people around me were slowly becoming aware of it, all because of one little sneaky find in my backpack. I didn't know whether that little accident would be the beginning of me getting better or worse. Would the depression now come back as bad as ever because my facade was falling apart? I was determined that it wouldn't. I didn't go back on my medication and decided I was going to rest over Christmas and start afresh in the New Year. The doctor said that it can take six weeks for the citalopram to

completely leave your system and for your natural serotonin levels to restore themselves. That meant that I
should be able to return after the Christmas break with
a new system, fresh oil, squeaky clean. Well, the serotonin
tank in my head must have had a frikin hole in it because
instead I became more and more miserable and struggled
to find peace in life without my tablets. I don't think I
was depressed, I just became lost again. I had that feeling
of being misplaced – the job wasn't me, it wasn't what
I was supposed to be doing. I hated being stuck in an
office – it was artificial, slaving away doing ten-hour days,
making someone rich and then having to ride the bus
home. It wasn't just the lack of money, it was the lack
of feeling alive – no fresh air, barely any daylight, 70 per
cent of conversations were about margins, rather than
about life in general. I'm not saying that we all need to
stop doing what we're doing and become hippies who
only talk about fixing the world's problems and focus on
love and spiritual growth, because the whole damn world
would stop. I'm just saying, I was slowly starting to realise
that it wasn't for me. This was progress – although, I
didn't know it at the time – I was starting to identify the
things in life that made me miserable. I just wanted to
feel happy again, whatever it took.

Just when I needed her most, Bryony had to leave to go
on tour with *Credible Likeable Superstar Role Model* in
Australia for four weeks. It was terrible timing. Having

her support was the only thing that was keeping me going without the tablets. It was a cold and miserable February. It was sub zero and devastatingly miserable in my head. When you're depressed you coil inside yourself; you avoid socialising and you leave yourself with the one thing you should avoid most: thoughts. Bryony was the only person I wanted to share them with and she wasn't there, so I dealt with them on my own. Or rather, I tried to deal with them on my own. Really I just drank. I started to drink a lot again and, of course, that didn't help one bit; it pushed me further down the brewery drain. Basically, I was self-medicating and, at the time, I thought it was better than being on those tablets. In reality, it's exactly the same – cloaking and drowning out the sorrow with a substance. I was still going to work but I wasn't happy; it was the last place I wanted to be but I thought, 'I gotta get that money.' One morning John asked to see me in the meeting room; it wasn't formal, we were mates and always had little one-on-ones, looking out for each other and watching each other's backs. We had worked side by side for almost five years so we were tight. He asked me how I was doing and I started crying in front of him. That was something I thought I'd never do. John's a typical alpha male: successful, smart and tough as a pair of old Bermondsey boxing gloves. He has a big heart, too, though, and I knew him well. I knew that under that macho cloak he was an emotional bloke. He could see the pain I was going through and it made him upset, and he welled up much like my dad did all those years earlier in my bedroom. It was one of those moments when two blokes are connected emotionally. It very rarely happens but it should. It feels good. It feels as though you know that you're both only human, life is hard at times and it's OK to talk about it.

Every time Bryony and I spoke over Skype I didn't want to put a downer on all the fun she was probably having so I put on a brave face and denied the way I was actually feeling. As the Skype chats went on, Bryony started to notice that I was melting away. She said my face was becoming gaunter and big dark circles were appearing under my miserable basset hound eyes. I didn't want to tell her how I felt because I didn't want to worry her, but the grim reaper himself had started floating into my life again. I couldn't understand it. On paper I should have been happy – good job, great girlfriend, loving family, amazing friends. But the paper doesn't mean shit. How you feel has nothing to do with what's on paper, it has everything to do with what's going on in your mind and whatever it was that was on my mind I couldn't shake off. My anxiety issues had calmed down but they seemed to have tag teamed the depression back into the ring. I woke up in the middle of the night and started to have suicidal thoughts again. I very clearly pictured myself hanging from our bedroom window. Just like I had with the treehouse tree a few years earlier. Why was

I hanging on both occasions? Why does there seem to be a preferred way of ending one's own life? I believe these thoughts aren't consciously constructed. They just happen. It's like the world's sneakiest reverse pickpocket places them there. Luckily for me they weren't strong enough to win the tug of war against team 'want to live'. But, nevertheless, it was still terrifying and made me think about going back on the medication.

Finally, Bryony arrived home and we had the first wobble in our relationship. The mix of jealousy, depression, tiredness and guilt all came to a head and we struggled for a short while. We were still madly in love but it felt like the extreme love bubble had been burst and now we were in reality and in a serious relationship. It probably wasn't the best time to tell her about the suicidal thoughts but I did anyway – I felt I had to. She got very upset and probably felt guilty that she hadn't been there to ease the pain. She shouldn't have felt any guilt, of course, and I explained that there was nothing she could have done and that her Skype reassurances were enough to keep me going until she got home. Having her back made me feel better instantly. It made me realise that part of the recent pain had been down to missing her – that heartache longing for someone when you feel half empty was partly to blame. However, even though she was back in my arms, I was still not myself. Plus there was the alarming fact that I had been having suicidal thoughts again.

D Diary
26th March – Feeling very low and not with it
27th March – Had feelings of a potential nervous breakdown and fear of going into work
28th March – Very low
29th March – Even worse today, don't want to talk. On the verge of tears all day
30th March – Broke down in tears
31st March – Broke down in tears at work, on the verge of crying all day, cried in the evening
1st April – Beginning to feel a little better, thinking about going back on meds.
2nd April – Started medication again

I had come off the meds cold turkey and it had failed. I had slowly weaned myself off them and that had also failed. Maybe I just couldn't be happy without them? I believed for so long that I was genuinely happy and that my happiness was a result of how well my life had been going – was I wrong? I had my ups and downs like everyone else but I was as happy as the next man. It had never occurred to me that it was actually the continued course of medication that was maintaining my happiness. I started to think about what genuine happiness was. Being on medication surely isn't 'genuine' happiness because it's partly artificial, I thought; it felt like I was putting a plaster over my problems. I just wanted to know if these tablets were hiding the real me. I concluded, at that point in time, that I was too unstable to be able to function at work without them and maybe it wasn't the right time to try to stop. I could always give it a go another time if I wanted to.

But this was good; I was admitting defeat and taking the meds again because I understood that I was ill and the wound needed urgent attention. This time, though, I started to think about ways of preventing the wound from opening again. Thinking more long term. What do I need to do to find genuine happiness, if that even exists?

Part of my wages went into a private health care fund for me. It meant I was covered by BUPA. I had been covered for roughly four years and it never occurred to me that I might be able to use it for my mental health and not just my physical health. One day a leaflet was sent around the office with details of the cover; there was a number on it and I called and asked if I was entitled to any therapy. I explained that I had been diagnosed with clinical depression five years earlier and that I'd only ever taken antidepressants and had never used therapy or counselling. They said that I was entitled to six sessions with a private CBT (cognitive behavioural therapy) therapist. I felt privileged that I could have it privately but after only three sessions I realized it wasn't for me. I was back on my medication and I think that had something to do with the clouding of what or where my problems were; the therapist and I didn't really know where to go. It was hard to explain how I felt when I was on antidepressants – they just made me go 'meh'. I felt like the therapy was a waste of time. Maybe we weren't the right match? Maybe I wasn't ready to listen properly? Maybe she was more interested in what she was having for dinner, who knows? All I know is that it wasn't right at the time. CBT is designed to tackle current problems or specific issues and can provide you with the daily tools to ease symptoms – which is why I think it can be good for anxiety – but the pills were already doing a great job keeping the anxiety at bay, so I didn't feel I needed the extra help. CBT breaks down your life into manageable and logical chunks – my problems weren't necessarily situational or in little chunks, they were something that needed pulling apart from the root and it would take time.

CHAPTER TWO

T: After I got ill again, seeing how worried you were
. . . made me sort of feel like a failure again, I guess.
And, er, I felt like I was back at the start basically.
Erm . . . dunno, I just thought that I was back to
being useless and I couldn't hack it and I wasn't
tough enough to get through it without the tablets
. . . And then, er, I thought that perhaps that's it for
ever . . . and I thought it might be better if I left you
to it.

I started to have my own private therapy sessions with
Bryony. We started to talk about what might be making
me so unhappy. It was more complicated than just one
single thing but there was something that played a big
part and we both knew what it was. I was spending ten
hours a day doing something that I didn't really enjoy
any more. I loved everyone I worked with; I just had no

real love for the job. I was very lucky to have it – not many people get to go to Brazil for five nights for free to drink mojitos and party on yachts and get paid for it. As amazing as all that was, it wasn't feeding my purpose or giving any meaning to my life. I kept hearing people say, 'If you're not happy then make some changes.' I hated that saying because I knew it was true but I didn't know where to start. I was too afraid to start. I didn't know what I was looking for. I realise now that the change doesn't have to be the perfect change, you don't have to wait until the right moment comes along because, more often than not, it never does. A change is a change no matter what it is. If it turns out to be the wrong one, then change it again. I had changed my diet and lifestyle but I wasn't unhappy with them in the first place; they were minor improvements that didn't really rattle my world. I knew the biggest thing I needed to do was change my job.

'Let's make a show together.'

Bryony's beautiful optimism that anyone can do anything was matched with my pessimistic, unconfident and stubborn refusal to even entertain the idea. We both wanted to spend more time with each other so it wasn't a bad idea but I had never done any performing or acting or public speaking or anything that involved me coming out of my shell artistically. After a while, I was so fed up and had completely failed to come up with any alternatives of my own so I started to come round to the idea. After showing her an inch of enthusiasm, she peppered me with ideas of what it could be about – everywhere we went, in the car, on the bus, in the pub, we talked about what the show could be. But we couldn't come up with anything that had legs. It was probably after a pub brainstorm that we decided we were going to make a comedy about our mutual love for Michael Jackson. We started making notes about stupid stuff we would do; I was delving right into the world of performance art now and I was intrigued. It seemed so free, nothing like I was used to. There were no rules, just complete freedom to explore. When we got serious and started talking about the potential of me quitting my job, the Jacko thing didn't seem to have enough meat. It wasn't a good enough idea for me to justify living without my salary.

We had a light bulb moment in the car one day and talked about doing a show about the unspoken epidemic of mental illness. We were finally moving in the right direction and agreed that it had to be something of substance, something that would make people think. Dressing up with white gloves and pretending to do the moonwalk wasn't going to do that.

When we talked about it some more, Bryony confessed that the fact I'd hidden my depression for so long really bothered her. She wanted to know why, like so many others, I felt ashamed of an illness that wasn't my fault. She was angry at the world for neglecting people who had depression, just because it was taboo. It wasn't something I'd ever really thought about – because I was one of them, I guess. I think she knew what had to be done long before she asked me. She wanted to make a show about my own experience. When she did finally get round to asking me, I flat out refused. Only my parents, my ex, John, Rod and Bryony really knew about my depression – I wasn't about to let the whole world know. The number of people who knew had grown from two to six in just a few months and I wanted to leave it at that. I wanted to be involved but I didn't want to use myself as an example; the thought of the exposure made me feel a bit sick. I've never been good at public speaking or being the centre of attention – I could barely speak in front of three people I knew in a meeting at work without shaking, there was no way I could perform on stage and talk about my problems in front of a bunch of strangers.

I slept on it and woke up with a new head and much bigger balls. I agreed to give it a go – hopefully we could convince people that hiding your problems and who you really are is not the way to do it. If it meant that I helped just one young person, then it'd be worth it. I thought about the younger me and how there was nothing that spoke about the subject honestly then. If there had been, I would have loved it and maybe it would have helped me. I also thought about all the doubters and the negative comments that we would inevitably receive. But then I thought, 'Fuck 'em.' I'm past caring what other people think. Also, to be honest, I was willing to do pretty much anything if it meant I could stop having to work in an office.

It was too soon to quit my job but we started to write things down and experiment in our spare time. Bryony got me to strip down to my pants in the living room so she could see what my body was like from a performer's perspective. She had me doing all sorts with my body, looking at me like a farmer about to buy some cattle. It was like she had discovered a caveman and was trying to make him a modern day man. I was so stiff, a long way off from being a performer. I found the whole process fascinating. From the day I met her, whenever anyone asked me what she did for a living, I'd say she was an artist who just pissed around all day. I had no idea how difficult it was to make something out of nothing. I also had no idea that to make something meaningful, you have to take on the responsibility of having to make someone not only think but feel. They need to feel emotions through your art, just like when you look at a painting or listen to a piece of music. It's a very compli-cated and layered process that derives from natural creativeness. We associate artists with being laidback but they put just as much pressure on themselves as any other professional.

We hadn't really spoken in depth about my experience of depression and we agreed that it was essential to know the full story before we started to write the show. I wasn't sure if I knew the full story myself. I had buried it all and had tried my damn hardest to forget about it. We decided to record ourselves chatting in our living room to see what we could take from it, not realising that it would become the backbone of our theatre show.

'Can you tell me a little bit about your childhood?'

That was the first question. I was reserved and rigid to begin with, like most people who have never had therapy. I'd never been asked that question before. We sat on the sofa for a couple of hours just talking and really opening up. I always thought I would be burdening people by talking about myself; I never felt like I deserved the time from someone else. Bryony made me feel the opposite. What started as quite a formal sort of interview became an intimate uncovering of both our souls. It was quite emotional and I think it was the first time Bryony realised the pain of what I had been feeling since I sent that email to work. She cried a lot and I kissed and cuddled her and tried to comfort her in the knowledge that I knew I'd be all right. I told her that I no longer felt the pain and hopelessness that I once had; it was a bit of a lie, looking back, I was still stuggling. However, I knew that I had made it through the worst and I was confident that my future was going to be better. I saw first-hand how much this new project meant to her and got quietly excited about what we were going to make together. That night we cooked some good food and watched a film. I said I'd always wanted to watch *Out of Africa* – I remember it being part of Dad's video collection but I'd never watched it. It had been on my List of Films To Watch for years, so we buckled down and sank into Robert Redford and Meryl Streep pissing about in the Ngong Hills. It was a sad but romantic film, a perfect reflection of the atmosphere in the room that night.

Over the next couple of weeks we tried to figure out how we could make a show about depression entertaining. We realised the sensitivity of the subject and found it difficult to balance humour and seriousness. We almost went back to the Michael Jackson idea but, as we talked more and more about my hidden past, it made us want to discover more about this strange taboo. We felt like journalists trying to uncover a hidden lab full of mentals being held against their will. I started to feel good, like someone had raised the dimmer switch ever so slightly. I had a surge of positivity every time we read a new article about mental health or had another idea for the show. It was like a drug I wanted more of. Every now and then my pessimism would interrupt and bring me back down, but Bryony was always there to take me back up. We were the perfect team – I had the catalogue and she had the rights to sell it.

The 2014 Edinburgh Fringe Festival was around the corner and it seemed like the perfect opportunity to put our idea of a show to the test. The only 'theatre' I had really seen before I met Bryony was a few *Punch and Judys*, and *Phantom of the Opera*. The theatre in Edinburgh was real theatre. I had taken a liking to this new world straightaway but I was still sceptical. Were people ready for a show about depression? Isn't a night out at the theatre supposed to be fun and an occasion to lift your spirits? Bryony and I agreed from the start that, even though the subject was depression and it would inevitably be sad, it also had to be fun and positive and not your stereotypical doom and gloom, violin-playing, dark hour of self-pity. We managed to get a spot at Forest Fringe: a small, not-for-profit space just outside of where all the commercial action is at the Edinburgh Fringe Festival. It's a great place that allows artists to perform and experiment with their work to non-paying audiences. We had two nights pencilled in. So, that was it, then; I was definitely going to perform at least twice in front of a hundred-strong audience.

If all went well in Edinburgh we were planning to tour the show in Australia at the Perth, Adelaide and Melbourne Fringe festivals. We started to work on the show in earnest, enthused by the prospect of sun and fun. We started experimenting in our living room one night a week in preparation. It was summertime so, if the weather was good, we'd go down to Hackney Downs in the evening and prance around there instead. Bryony said that she wanted the show to look like a safari camp in the early twentieth century, just like *Out of Africa*. That was that, then. I didn't question it, I knew some-where in that head of hers it made sense.

I sat her down before we really got started and expressed my concerns about how I would crumble from nervousness. I thought that I would survive for much longer if I couldn't see the hundred sets of eyeballs staring back at me. Bryony came up with a solution – I could wear various hats and objects that shielded my line of vision from the audience. Fine by me. It was amazing how flexible it all was; literally no idea was a bad idea. I was still getting used to working without a rulebook. We made dances and wrote songs. I was in complete awe of Bryony's ability to create things out of nothing and she was in hysterics at my Bambi-on-ice balance and performing composure.

We were a week away from our first-ever performance and we had only written thirty minutes of material for a show that was supposed to be sixty minutes long. This didn't help my anxiety and nervousness one little bit, and there were moments when I looked in the mirror and said to myself that I was an idiot and I couldn't do it. I was still working and no one in the office knew what I was doing in my spare time. Forest Fringe was pretty low key, so there wasn't much chance of seeing anyone I knew or anyone hearing about it, so I just pretended I was going to be on holiday. In that week building up to it, I went home and worked on the show with Bryony every night until we had our sixty minutes. I thought that the material needed to be polished and finished before we could even think about performing it, but Bryony told me that this was the process and there would never be a 'finished show'. She was right; in the end, every show was different. I hated the idea of not being completely happy with it, though; I wanted it to be perfect before anyone saw it. Thankfully the performance art scene is open to absolutely anything. Everyone in it, from the Arts Council to the audience members, encourages any form of artistic exploration. I think that was why I had managed to pluck up the courage to give it a go – the whole scene was so relaxed and inviting that the majority of my nerves were extinguished.

That is, until I found myself in the dressing room dressed as a shoddy Robert Redford absolutely shitting myself at the prospect of standing in front of all those people and telling them that I was depressed. The nerves were back in full force. What the fuck was I doing? Once again I thought about the younger me who may be in the audience and I remembered that I wasn't doing it for me now – I was doing it for him and I needed to let him know that he was not alone. I walked behind the stage and I could hear the pre-theatre footsteps and voices of the hundred people as they found their seats. Bryony stood in the middle of the stage waiting to introduce the show casually and let them know that it was a work in progress and by no means a finished piece of theatre.

'It's Tim's first ever time on stage.'

This was met with a round of applause, which eased the nerves by 0.05 per cent. The room fell quiet and my heart started to race, the sound of it beating was the only thing I could hear as I waited for my cue to come on. All I had to do was walk slowly into the middle of the stage when the music from *Out of Africa* started playing. I shook so badly with every step that everyone in the audience must have noticed. The room was silent. It was the most exposed I had ever been in my life. Throughout the show I forgot my words and was never in the right position on stage but we got through it. It was kind of a shambles, but the intensity and unity in the room made it something I'll never forget. It was like every single one of us realised that we knew someone who was going through the same thing and it was ridiculous that we weren't all talking about it. It was a huge relief when the lights went down and in an instant I felt the main weight of all those years crumble down my shoulders. Bryony cried, I cried and every single audience member cried. It was a peaceful, beautiful atmosphere that I had never experienced before and probably never will again. Not sad or hopeless but the exact opposite – the room felt happy and hopeful. We had all laughed and cried for an hour and were in a yo-yo of smiles and tears. It was the most collective emotional experience I had ever been a part of. We saw how art could be the tool to bring people together and make them feel each other's problems. We're too often soaked up in our own lives to feel touched by other people's problems and the show felt like it sucked out emotions and feelings that the audience members didn't know they had in them, ones they were only too willing to share. Without realising it, the competent prowess of Bryony's performance combined with my vulnerable nervousness gave the show its perfect balance.

The second night was much the same. I was still a nervous wreck and struggled to remember my lines or compose myself on stage. Again, before the show started Bryony reminded the audience that I really worked in advertising and had only ever been on stage once before. I hated the idea of people feeling sorry for me but I needed it. I preferred that to a stiff, critical audience. Bryony and I worked all day before the show, trying to polish some of the mistakes we had made the night before and add to some scenes that we thought were lacking finesse. There wasn't a smidgen of finesse in the whole thing but we tried anyway. The response from the audience was fantastic again, but the connection and emotional atmosphere wasn't the same as it had been on the first night. We came close. That second night we realised that the rawness and real-life aspect of the first night was what people loved. It was a nod to the subject of depression; depression *is* real life. The fusion of that real life on a magical, anything-goes stage really worked. We realised that to expose the taboo we just had to confront it head on, even if it made us look vulnerable.

I don't think anyone could quite believe that no one had done this before. Why wasn't everyone talking about this subject that kills so many people? It was obvious by the end of the weekend that people wanted us to make this into a full production. Both nights there had been all sorts of people from the Arts in the audience, people with the purse strings to help us do it, and producers who wanted to help us make it. The weekend felt like a real success; we could head home to London with a real reason for me to quit my job.

We woke up the next morning and turned the TV on. Robin Williams had died. Together with most of the rest of the world we were in shock. All the headlines were saying that depression had led him to commit suicide. This was the first high-profile news story of its kind that I had ever seen and it happened one day after I'd been on stage spilling my own experiences of suicidal thoughts. It was another hint that this was something we had to do. For weeks the news about Robin Williams was the topic of a lot of conversations. I heard people talking about it everywhere I went. 'But he had so much money and a great career.' 'What did he have to be depressed about?' 'He was hilarious; how could he have been depressed?' It was great that people were talking about depression so openly and it was also great that people were starting to ask questions about what depression really was. It was another one of those moments when something really bad has to happen in order to open people's eyes. If it had been a famously miserable, sad, violent, addicted celebrity then people may have just associated those personality traits with suicide and it wouldn't have caused such a stir. But this was a funny man, a seemingly glass-half-full sort of person; it was big news. Being an

A-list celebrity also made it big news, of course. It is sad that it took Robin Williams to die for depression to make the news – someone dies by suicide every 40 seconds of every day and you never hear about it. The more I heard people talking about it, though, the more confident I was that our little show might work. People wanted to know more.

I had tried to keep the performance art world as separate from my work and social life as possible. But after Edinburgh it became a little more difficult. I started to tell a selected few people what I was up to. All my closest mates were really happy for me and didn't treat me any differently. Nowadays I can talk about it with as much ease as a conversation about what I had for breakfast, but I'm pretty sure the fear of exclusion or ridicule was there at the beginning. I was worried about what people would think but I was also confident that we were about to do something proper, something that meant something, and I knew this would connect to real people. At one point, some doughnut said to me, 'Depression doesn't exist, babes. What have you got to be depressed about?' Idiots like that can't be left to carry on thinking that way – 'We have to do the show,' I thought to myself. We need to reach as many people as possible with the message that mental illness is real, regardless of age, gender, sexuality, race and class. Idiots will, of course, continue to be ignorant, but it was time to decide what team I was going to be on – that narrow-minded fool's, or the team of people who stood up for the truth, who want to experience and understand things outside their own world.

I sat at work patiently waiting for Bryony's email to pop into my inbox; the email that would confirm we had the cash to tour *Fake It 'Til You Make It* in Australia. I had my resignation email already written and it was sitting in my drafts folder ready to release.

New message from Bryony: 'We're in, we leave 26th Jan.'

I was so excited; I was finally doing something I gave a shit about. I sent that resignation email to my seniors at work and it was official – I was leaving my career to go on the road with a theatre show about my depression. Weird how things turn out. Word got around the office that I was leaving. I told everyone I liked the real reason why I was leaving and they were supportive and made me feel like I had made the right decision. Anyone I didn't really know, I just said that I was going travelling. I wasn't ready to tell colleagues who I barely knew that I had been clinically depressed for five years and that was why I was jacking in my career. I wish I had done now; the awkward silence would have been funny. Over time my lack of caring what other people thought picked up. The success of the 'work in progress' shows at Edinburgh and the financial backing gave me the confidence to talk about the show more openly. I still had a way to go before

I could talk about my own situation with ease and, if I ever did talk about it, I usually referred to my problems in the past tense. People took to the conversation more when they knew that it was a going to be a real show and not just a performance in my living room. I started to tell clients and people I met for business lunches and the more positive reactions I got, the more I wanted to tell everyone. It felt so good; I was beginning to become loud and proud about who I was and it sparked some meaningful conversations and debates about the whole world of mental illness. People wanted to know more and contributed to conversations with their own stories or feelings about the subject. It was time to enjoy my notice period and the people I had worked with for almost five years. It was the happiest I had been for a long time.

I booked a cheeky little holiday to Rome for me and Bryony. We left the day after my last day at work – 31 October 2014. I had planned the holiday for quite a while and we were booked into a beautiful flat overlooking the flower market Campo de' Fiori. It was perfect. We walked around the city on our first day there just taking it all in and casually drinking and eating wherever we went. I knew that I wanted to marry Bryony and this felt like the perfect time to ask if she was up for it. I wasn't nervous at all until the very moment I asked her. I've spoken to a lot of blokes who felt the same. It's something you've planned for a long time and everything is under control until you get down on that knee and you're looking up at the person you love most in the whole world and you lose your shit. Just dribble came out of my mouth. She said yes and we celebrated with champagne and sex. We were now a proper team. We were going to be working together and we were engaged.

As soon as we got back from Rome, it was time to get started on making the show full time – we had three months, with Christmas in the middle. We had managed to raise around £30k to make the show, thanks to the Arts Council, Theatre Works, Dance Exchange, the Southbank Centre, Soho Theatre and the amazing, generous, normal human beings who supported our Kickstarter. Other than Bryony, the most instrumental person in making it all happen was our producer Dan Clarke from Theatre Works in Australia. He had taken *Credible Likeable Superstar Role Model* to Australia the year before and that had been a big success, so he worked really hard to get *Fake It* over there, too. Dan is one of the most brilliant people I've ever met. He's a big gay man with a huge heart and is full of energy. He's married to a great guy called Nick and I love them both. The money we received had to cover rental space to rehearse, costumes, technical support and loads of other hidden costs I had no idea about. We weren't exactly rolling in it and I had taken a huge pay cut, more than half my previous salary, but I can honestly say I never felt the difference.

First off we had a week booked in a dance studio in Bristol to work on my dance skills. It was pretty cool – one week I was sitting at my computer looking at spread sheets, the next I was dancing around in a studio and getting paid for it. All that money I had earned previously, I realise I had spent it pointlessly on material things to try and make me happy – as happy as I now was dancing around like a ballerina.

I was still pretty emotionally unstable, though, and still taking the tablets. I was a rigid thirty-one-year-old businessman who needed breaking down and flexing out. I was very reserved and didn't want to make a tit of myself and that was something that Bryony knew had to go; she knew that, in order to really connect with the story and the audience, I had to drop my guard. Our dance teacher got me to do an exercise where I was blindfolded and made to do a freestyle dance to some music. The music was very slow and sad and didn't give you much to work with in terms of movement. That was the point; it made you work really hard to force creative movement out of yourself. I was embarrassed to do it in front of two people, and one of them was my fiancée – there was a lot of work to be done if I was ever going to be able to do it in front of big audiences. After a few attempts ruined by nervous laughter, I finally did it and I felt as if I'd gone into a different universe. It was like a form of meditation, where all my stresses and worries and insecurities disappeared. I was properly expressing myself without saying a word. It was something so far removed from my normal life and I was breaking down the macho barrier protecting what I thought were my weaknesses. I took the blindfold off and cried uncontrollably; I was extremely emotional and it felt out of my control. The bastards had opened the lid and it poured out of me like a bad spirit that had been locked inside for too long. This was the next big step in coming to terms with my depression. It was OK to cry if I felt I needed to.

After five days in Bristol it was safe to say that I wasn't going to be the next MJ. However, it was a good first step in flexing me out and getting some rough choreography sorted. We knew we wanted to do an old-fashioned dance at some point in the show – I think we just wanted to show how much we were in love by doing a romantic little waltz. At the beginning I had very little creative opinion, I just went with what the pro said. It was a good start but it was just the beginning. I asked Bryony if I could learn to play the guitar because, if I was going to be on stage performing, I wanted to be good at something and dancing wasn't going to be it. I actually wanted to learn the drums but we realised it wasn't practical to tour Australia with a drum kit in tow so we went with guitar lessons. I had two or three lessons with Tom Parkinson, a good friend of Bryony's – he's the amazingly musically talented bloke who wrote, produced and recorded the music for the show. He's incredible to watch; he can pick up any object and make music out of it – even babies. The two of them are a great team and have worked on loads of projects together and still do. Tom took about seven minutes to write a song out of thin air and started to teach me how to play it. We weren't quite sure when it would feature in the show and it really depended on how good I could get. If I was a natural, maybe I could have played a few songs. Turns out I wasn't and we decided to stick to just one – one song that I would play at the end of the show as a kind of serenade to Bryony and a final stand to my nervousness. While I was trying to become some sort of artist, Bryony was churning out all sorts of ideas for the script and the direction the show could take. It was exciting and different and every day felt like a mini adventure.

At the start of December we had a couple of weeks off as Bryony had another project she needed to work on and she had to put some time into that. I went and worked for a builder mate of mine knocking down walls and shit to get some extra pocket money. Once those two weeks were done, we started a week-long workshop in Chats Palace. A workshop is basically a brainstorm. We developed the show and tried to reach those 60 minutes of polished material. On the last day of the workshop we invited twenty-five people to come and watch what we had done so far. Among the twenty-five were Bryony's family, a few of our friends, a few people from the companies who had backed us and a couple of the people who had donated to our Kickstarter. I didn't want my family to see it until it was completely finished and we had toured Australia. I don't know why; I think I just wanted them to see it at its best. They understood and were cool with it. The preview went well and we got some good feedback. It had come a long way since Forest Fringe but there were still mountains to climb. It was an amazing process, really, just experimenting and trying loads of things out. I wasn't very good at improvising in front of audiences, I always wanted to play it safe but Bryony pushed the limits every time and I guess that's why she's very good at what she does. Most of the good stuff we ended up with started out of nothing. Nearly every show we performed was different – by the last twenty-five or so, they started to be the same as we were finally happy by then. Up until that point, though, we had all sorts of different scenes and dances and jokes that we included or gradually deleted over time because we didn't feel they were good enough.

Christmas was fast approaching and Bryony suggested that I take a little time off, as I hadn't stopped since I left Maxus, plus she had loads of other work to do. I went to the gym and watched films and generally just chilled and looked after myself. I thought about what I was doing and for the first time in my life I felt proud of myself. It was the first time in a long time that I had the time to think properly and I thought about my previous attempts to come off my medication and all the mistakes I had made in doing so. I had never really given it my all, or had the time to see through the withdrawal period. It had always got too much because of work. Now I didn't have the pressures of a nine-to-five job, could I do it? I booked an appointment with the doctor and talked about coming off the tablets again. I thought that Australia would be a good place to start – it was sunny, I was going to be busy, and I would be with Bryony 24/7. The doctor disagreed and said that because everything was changing so much it wasn't a good time to unsettle the balance, plus we were a couple of weeks away from Christmas and why would I want to ruin Christmas? I saw where she was coming from but decided to go against her advice and drop my dose from 30mg to 20mg on Christmas day. I remember feeling fine over Christmas and then I had a little wobble over New Year and the few days that followed, but I knew that it was a slight adjustment while my nut got used to 20mg again. After a week or so of not being sure whether it was a good idea, I balanced out and felt much better than I had before Christmas. The trusty 20mg dose had my back.

Christmas and New Year passed and we were fast approaching the time to fly out to Australia. We still had loads to do on the show and it was nowhere near finished – even Bryony leaked out a little concern. She was pretty stressed but was confident we would get it done. She said that even if we didn't get it right before we left, we had all of Australia to get it right before my family saw it in London. I had learnt not to get stressed by how casual it was; I trusted her. I didn't have a choice – we were two weeks away from flying out. We had a week booked in a studio in Oxford, followed by a week booked in the Hackney Empire where, by the end of the week, we would do one last 'sharing', and then actual humans with actual money would come to see our little show on the other side of the planet.

CHAPTER THREE

B: *This is Tim Grayburn, up close and personal in his pants. He is a man, a real man, the strong and silent type.*

We flew out to Perth, Western Australia, on 26 January. We left Heathrow knowing that we still had a bit of work to do to get the show to where we wanted it to be. In between looking into each other's eyes and not quite believing that we were really doing it, Bryony wrote for most of the first leg to Dubai. There wasn't much I could do but run a few lines and watch films, so I pestered her for almost twelve hours to have sex in the toilets but she was having none of it. Alas, even though I didn't join the weird club of people who've had sex where millions shit, it was pretty exciting times. I was on a plane on my way to tour a theatre show about my battles with depression and anxiety to thousands of

Australians – exciting but terrifying at the same time. We had a pint at Dubai airport and cheered each other while I pretended to listen to Bryony's amendments to the show. Really I was watching the football over her shoulder. What an arsehole. We were so happy and felt very lucky and couldn't wait to get there.

We arrived in Perth two days after we left London. A really nice bubbly girl sent from the Perth Institute of Contemporary Arts picked us up from the airport and took us to what was to be our house for two weeks. It was perfect and Perth looked like something out of *The Truman Show*. White picket fences everywhere, everything was pristine and all the people looked healthy and happy. It was a far cry from the grey, gloomy, miserable, wintry London that we'd left behind. There wasn't much time to rest and get over the jet lag, though; we had two days before we were going to perform our finished-on-a-plane show at the beautiful waterside Mandurah Performing Arts Centre. Mandurah had been added to the diary at the last minute – it wasn't part of the Fringe World Festival but it gave us an opportunity to a) practise and b) see what the Australians thought of this English boy and his girlfriend talking about depression so openly. It was quite a stressful couple of days, to be fair. Bryony was a little tense as a lot of the responsibility to make the show great fell on her shoulders and that, coupled with my lack of sleep, induced a general low mood and sense of anxiety, which didn't make it an enjoyable arrival in Perth. The day before our first show in Mandurah, I remember rehearsing in the garden of the house in the morning, inside in the air con over lunch and then back in the garden when the sun had chilled out a bit. I remember sitting under the veranda, bare feet touching the spiky grass, practising my guitar and soaking up the warm evening atmosphere. I thought to myself, 'This is just my journey – that is all.' I usually try to romanticise every moment, picture myself in a film, but this time I was in touch with reality. It was romantic in a real sense; it was the beginning of a story, a journey that I was in control of. This was it; right there and then, the film of my life. I felt I was ready. I left the majority of my nerves in that garden and woke up the next morning full of optimism.

On our way to Mandurah, we stopped off in Perth and had our first live radio interview. We were well looked after and made to feel a bit special. The presenters were real cool and we talked about the show for about ten minutes. They were so amazed by the fact that I had quit my job to do this and it made me feel like the hype created by such a drastic measure to do something about the stigma of mental illness could really pick up pace. After that interview we were put in a car and driven to do a TV interview for the evening news. I must admit it felt pretty good. I felt like Beyoncé being driven around all over the place. I had no idea beforehand but it turns out the media had heard about the show and wanted to cover it. I remember thinking, 'You haven't even seen it yet; don't big it up too much!' After the TV interview we were thrown in another car and driven the hour and a half down the coast to Mandurah. We had a few hours to 'tech' before showtime. Tech means getting the show technically ready: lights, sound, props etc. It takes a long time and it was the most stressful thing about the whole experience for me. I didn't have a clue what I was doing, so was mainly used as a prop to stand in certain places to see if the stage was lit properly. You only have an allocated amount of time and we had a lot to do. We had quite a complicated set up where we erect a tent during the show. It's achieved with pullies and lots of rope, and was designed to look as though we were doing it ourselves, without actually having to fumble around with tent poles. Anyway, it meant a lot of adjusting and untangling of ropes; it took a long time and stressed me out.

We both sat in the dressing room afterwards feeling pretty tense. We didn't have much time after the frantic tech to compose ourselves. The theatre started to fill with the audience and we were told we had fifteen minutes until showtime. We were in our costumes but we weren't ready to do this. We hadn't had time to do a run through; we were just going to have to go with what we knew. Bryony told me not to worry and to remember that this was really just a practice before the real festival started. I remember feeling pretty worried about how it would go down with the audience. I hadn't even thought about it until that moment, but I remembered that I'd read somewhere that Australian men, in general, were typically backwards in terms of emotional expressiveness. A theatre show about a bloke whining about his depression was a big risk. I kept picturing Mick Dundee throwing a tin of beans at my head. However, as much as I was worried about big, macho, Aussie dudes calling me a pussy, I was determined to stand up for those same blokes who were most likely suffering from depression themselves. Before we left the UK we had done a bit of research into mental health in Australia and we'd learnt that men make up 75 per cent of all suicides in Australia and, like in the UK, there's a big problem with most of them being undiagnosed or untreated cases of depression. The main reason for this was denial or shame – a refusal to accept or confront their problems. It was particularly bad at the time in Western Australia because there was a boom in the mining industry and a lot of young men were regularly away from home, putting them in isolation from their families and other social supports. They were working long hours for weeks at a time and getting no sunlight. Drugs were a big problem, too, particularly the easily attainable meth, or 'Ice' as they call it. Understandably, all these factors have a significant effect on one's mental health. This knowledge gave me faith that what I was about to do was important.

The lights went down and we stepped out for the first time in front of a paying audience. I was nervous but nowhere near as nervous as I had been in Edinburgh. I could feel that it was going to get easier and easier every time I did it. The theatre was half full, around fifty to seventy-five people, and the show started really well; we were getting laughs and the audience seemed as if they were engaged. We got to the part where we erect the tent and it was a disaster. The pullies didn't work properly and it was back to front. Fucking tent. Bryony just muttered under her breath to carry on and we continued as if it had miraculously floated up and positioned itself all on its own. There were a few other mistakes but we managed to get through it and felt that the rawness and clunky style still spoke to the audience in a good way, a human way. At the end they all stood up, some crying and some shaking their heads with buttoned lips in that amazed and respectful way. After the show, one woman told me that three guys had committed suicide in her company alone in the past six months. Already the stuff we had read about was proving to be true and the more time we spent in Perth, with the radio chats about mental health, the more evident it became that men's mental health, in particular, was a big problem there. After we had packed up the set and changed out of our costumes, the artistic director bought us a beer and we talked about the show and mental health in general. It was a big relief to have that first show behind us but we knew we still had some work to do. I went outside for a cigarette and someone who was in the audience came up and shook my hand and thanked me for my honesty. I could see that it meant a lot to him and it made it all worth it. Maybe I won't burn that tent, I thought. The following night was much the same, albeit slightly more polished, and I requested at least an hour before the show started to make sure the tent ran smoothly. It did this time and the show was an improvement on the night before. We had the same reaction from the audience and, again, it felt good. It was a Sunday and we went back to the house for some well-deserved Sunday rest. We only had one day off before the festival started on the Tuesday.

We walked around Fringe World soaking up the atmosphere and I saw our name in big letters on a poster listing the show times at the PICA theatre in the heart of Perth. It was exciting and I actually couldn't wait to get started. In the few hours leading up to the first show we had to do tech again; you have to do it at every new venue. I hated it because it was the only time Bryony and I bickered. Anyway, we smashed it out and went backstage to get ready. I think the radio and TV coverage helped get in numbers because the theatre was almost full; there were only around twenty to thirty empty seats out of a hundred-odd capacity. We felt good and we were so glad we had done the two nights in Madurah before starting the five nights at the festival. The show went really well and it was the best we had done yet; neither of us put a foot wrong. There was still some polishing to do on the dances and my guitar playing, but we were pretty happy with it. We went out and celebrated and met some great people – other artists, audiences, people who work for the theatres and the festival. The atmosphere was immense; it was summer nights mixed with art, alcohol and good times. It was alive. Everywhere you looked there was something going on. I loved it. Bryony was hugely connected in that world and knew pretty much everyone. It was nice because I just went with the flow and got to go and see all sorts of brilliant shows – comedy, circus shows and theatre shows. I'd never seen so much art in my life and it was great.

To help fund *Fake It 'Til You Make It*, Bryony had to perform a back catalogue of her hugely successful show *Sex Idiot*. It was one she had written three years previously and was a solo show. She had to perform that as a financial safety net in case *Fake It* was a flop. It turned out that *Fake It* was just as, if not more, successful than *Sex Idiot*. While she was doing the solo show, I hung out with a guy called Chip, who had his own show that ran just before ours on the same stage. We were like kids and pissed around in the bar, or I'd go and see shows on my own while Bryony performed. I used to get jealous of Bryony doing her show and I regret it. I don't know if it was the subject matter or Bryony using it to keep me on my toes but I wasn't as comfortable with it as I would be now. I guess I was a little insecure. The show is about how she contracted an STI and went back to talk to all her old sexual partners about it. Apparently it's brilliant, I've still never seen it and probably never will. Anyway, it wasn't a huge deal and I'd swing by and pick her up afterwards and we'd go and meet friends and have a few drinks.

The little show of ours, though, started to get a lot of attention. It was funny how it gathered momentum as the days went on. The numbers in the audience started to grow, we started to get quite a lot of press coverage in the local newspapers and then reviews started pouring in. The positive reactions made us work hard at getting the show even better. By the end of the week we were sold out and receiving standing ovations. We were having a great time – we were on the beach in the day and doing the show at night. The pressure of the show being successful had started to ease. With two nights to go we were told that we had been nominated for 'Best Theatre Award'. There were approximately 500 shows happening at the festival, some with huge production teams and big casts, and Bryony, the talented solo performance artist, and her dopey depressed ad man boyfriend had been nominated! Pretty sweet. Because of the hype during the week and because, by the last few shows, we were sold out with huge reserve lists of people wanting to see the show, we thought that maybe we had a chance, but we didn't pin any hopes on it. Just after finishing our last show, we were told that we had won it! We were well chuffed. We celebrated with all the lovely lot at PICA and my new best bud Chip. This was a real confidence boost and made me look forward to doing more shows and maybe winning more awards. I loved this new life on the road and didn't want it to end.

Even though I was reminded about my mental health every day with the show, I didn't think about it once.

We flew to Adelaide, on the back of our success in Perth, to start the three-week-long run at their Fringe Festival: the biggest in the southern hemisphere and second largest in the world after Edinburgh. Just over 4,000 artists performed in 900-odd shows over the three weeks, so there was a lot more competition for ticket sales and awards. We were completely over the jetlag by then and had settled down after that hectic first week in Australia. After the win in Perth, the nerves and uncertainty had disappeared. We seemed to get more hype, because of the success in Perth, and it began to feel like we were local festival celebrities, which was weird. Bryony loved it and soaked it all up – rightly so, she had been working in this industry for a while and had worked hard to get to this point of success, so she deserved it. I found it a little strange seeing myself in the papers with headlines like, 'He was suicidal, she saved him' but enjoyed the ride anyway. As the media attention picked up with front-page news stories and TV interviews, it felt that we, along with some other great acts, had really become part of a movement to promote men's mental health in Australia. It felt great to be a part of the positivity that was bubbling up. The only downside was that now it felt like we had a lot to live up to. We didn't panic, though, and just continued to do the show and enjoy sharing that hour with new faces every night.

I had a great time in Adelaide; Bryony was getting burnt out a bit – she still had to do *Sex Idiot* as well as *Fake It* so she was working really hard and I felt a little guilty that I could chill out after our show and she couldn't. After the first week or so she got used to it and we began to feel settled. We had never taken our stuff out of the suitcase in Perth but we had almost a month in Adelaide, so we properly unpacked and made ourselves at home in our apartment. We had a couple of bikes and loved exploring the place in the 40-degree heat. The whole place was buzzing; people from Adelaide told us that every year during February and March they cram all the excitement of the annual calendar into two months and then the place goes quiet until the following year. They had the Fringe on, some racing event, international cricket and a couple of music festivals. The streets were constantly full of people enjoying themselves; I loved it. We also met some great people and it felt like one big carnival family.

Our theatre was more like a big circus tent with a capacity of about 250. It was the biggest space we had performed in so far. There were so many shows going on and so much competition for ticket sales that we weren't sure we'd sell out, even after our win in Perth. We had a little portable cabin to use as our dressing room with a shower tent – all the acts in our garden had the same and each one was placed around the perimeter of the garden. Some of my favourite memories of that time are from sitting outside our cabin with everyone else in the evening sun preparing for our shows and wishing each other good luck, all of us knowing that we'd have an ice cold beer waiting for us at the end. As we prepared for our first show in Adelaide, Bryony said she thought it would be good to have the audience feel part of the show themselves. She didn't want them just to watch someone else's story and then leave with their own experiences kept all to themselves. She came up with the idea of inviting people to share their stories, as a kind of after-show care.

B: *Well that was our love story. Sorry, gross. But we also recognise that it may be some of your stories, too. And, if that is the case, we'd like to take this moment at the end of the show to say: tonight you have met two fellow members of your tribe. And if you ever wanted to email us then all of our details can be found on your free sheets or at Bryony and Tim dot com. Thanks for coming to our show.*

The emails started to flood in and every night we'd get around twenty from all sorts of people: people who were extremely troubled, people who were in love with someone with a mental health problem and didn't know what to do, doctors, mums, dads, brothers, sisters and teachers. In all we received 205 emails and I wrote back to every single one. I've kept them as a kind of literature trophy. It was fascinating to see the connection between us all; mental health really does affect every single one of us in some way. Some stories were heartbreakingly sad; especially the ones about people who had lost someone through suicide. They were hard to read. But none of them was negative. They were hopeful. Out of all of them, there was one that really stuck in my mind and made me happy. I don't know what it is about this one but it was concise and honest and I imagined him to be just like my younger self. It reminded me why I was doing the show:

Hi Tim,

I came to see 'Fake It 'Til You Make It' recently in Adelaide and felt the need to send you an email thanking you for your courage. The morning after the performance I went to my GP and have been diagnosed with depression anxiety disorder, which I am now receiving treatment for. I was moved to tears several times during your performance and your honesty and courage enabled me to summon the inner strength to face and challenge my own demons. You are both also fucking hilarious and, diagnosis aside, the show was bloody brilliant. Well done and keep up the good work.

Thanks
Stuart

I still think about Stuart. I wonder about who he is, what he looks like, what his story is, what may have happened to him if he hadn't seen the show. Wherever and whoever he is, I hope he's doing well and I want to thank him for making my time in Adelaide great. Adelaide *was* great. It felt like a carnival atmosphere every day with people everywhere just having fun and watching shows. I absolutely loved it. It was the perfect job, meeting new people, cycling around a new city, stopping off for a beer here and there, swimming in the sea and then doing an hour's show of what felt like therapy in front of a 250-strong audience. After every show I felt myself changing; my insecurities, worries and pessimism were all slowly being knocked down. I imagine what I was feeling was similar to what someone feels as they walk out of a particularly good therapy session – a release of fear and anxiety, a clean slate, nothing to hide, confident and content with who they are. I felt so liberated from my old life that it injected a hope of true happiness into me. I could finally see through the dark cloud and knew that my depression didn't have to be with me for the rest of my life. I knew I wanted to find out what true happiness was, not just settle for 'on the surface' happy. I wanted to find and keep a deep-rooted happiness and I was going to do it if it was the last thing I did. Of course, happiness isn't just a precious stone you find and then that's it, you never need to worry about being unhappy again. I know it's not that simple. You can lose it; it can crack. I did realise this, but somehow I knew that it would be possible to find it again or find another kind of happiness. Hope replaced the hopelessness I had been living with for five years and I felt I now lived with purpose. I didn't sign up to do the show knowing that would be how I ended up feeling; the discovery of this realisation was part of the elation. Things just started getting better and better. We began selling out every show, some a few days in advance, and we started to get more five-star reviews. Every day was like this for three weeks – perfect. Nothing could top it off. Until it did.

On 14 March, the day before our very last show in Adelaide, Bryony woke me up by waving a pregnancy test over my eyes. Four weeks PREGNANT. It was the best news I'd ever had. I jumped up and celebrated like it was 1999 (when Man United won the Champions League final against Bayern Munich). Our child had entered the universe; he was a spark that was created by the two of us at the pinnacle of our happiness and, well, I couldn't have been happier. I remember Bryony being very quiet and reserved about how she felt. It was what she wanted – it was what we both wanted – but it was as if she wanted to nest immediately and her love for the tour and Australia ended that morning. It wasn't the same for her after that and I could tell she no longer wanted to be there. I'm pretty sure I asked her what was wrong and I don't think she was honest with me – she didn't want to ruin the happiness I felt. I pretended to accept that 'nothing was wrong' but I knew that she didn't want to be living out of a bag, no matter how pregnant she was.

The next day we got ready for our final show of the festival. We were heading to Melbourne next but, before we got there, we had to go to the closing party and award ceremony for the Adelaide Festival. We had been nominated for Best Theatre Award again but we weren't feeling too optimistic about winning it this time. There was some big competition from fantastic high-budget shows. As they read out the nominations, I thought about how my life had changed so much in so little time and that standing next to me was my fiancée and unborn child and things were continuously getting better – all because she found those tablets. I decided there and then that there would never be a better time for me to come off the medication. Maybe it would be third time lucky. I had nine months to get myself the healthiest and happiest I could be – I wanted my A game in the room when I met my little hero. I didn't need the tablets. I could see my future and it was stable and mental-health friendly. I can't explain the clarity I had, but I suddenly knew that I didn't need them any more; it's like when a toddler realises they don't need their dummy. It's only you who can truly decide whether you're ready or not. I felt strong enough and clear enough to live my life without them; I just knew it. Obviously I couldn't see the actual future and there was a hint of 'what ifs' but I knew that I was ready to give it a go. As I shook hands with the devil of depression to seal the deal, Dan screamed, 'We won!' I turned around and he was crying. He was so over-whelmed and all the emotions from the last couple of months came to a head. It was time to celebrate the deal! It was the proudest moment of my life. I remember embarrassingly saying to everyone who congratulated me that I never win anything – but it was true; I had never won anything like this. Once again I felt really proud of myself. For all those years, my depression had made me feel self-doubt and worthless – now it was winning me awards.

Next stop was the Melbourne International Comedy Festival. I had always wanted to go to Melbourne, so I was looking forward to checking it out and watching some comedy. I make it sound like it was all just a laugh – it wasn't. It was hard work and tiring and doing so many shows back-to-back does take its toll on you, espe-cially when you're pregnant and technically depressed. Bryony started to get the dreaded sickness and really didn't want to do it any more. Jumping around on stage late at night is not what a pregnant woman should be doing. To be fair to her, though, she put on a brave face and did the show every night for three weeks, sometimes almost throwing up right before the curtains opened. I still had the 'life as a travelling artist' bug but the fact that Bryony was having a tough time and not really wanting to be there made it less enjoyable than Perth or Adelaide. I felt her pain and just tried to be on hand to make it as easy as I could for her. Nothing really helped. She just wanted to get home and cook our little baby up – in her stomach, of course. That suited me, really, and kind of encouraged the beginning of my 'third time lucky' plan. I didn't want to go out drinking all night when Bryony was home feeling sick and baby poisoned, so I started to exercise properly again and began to look after myself, like a boxer getting ready for a big fight. I joined the gym and went on long runs down the coast of south Melbourne. I loved the lifestyle over there, every day at 5:30pm the beach was full of people hanging out with each other, chilling on their own, reading a book, unwinding after a day at work, or kite surfing in the sea. It was a positive environment to be in to encourage myself to get fit and ready. I wanted to be off the tablets, happy and stable by the time the baby came, so I did my calculations – I figured that I had four months of reducing by 5mg each month: 15mg, 10mg, 5mg, 2.5mg. If I could do that then it would give me six weeks with no medication to assess how mental I was. So I would have six weeks to get my brain back to happy, sane, baby-caring mode. Bryony was worried that if the master plan went pear-shaped then she was going to be left to look after a newborn baby and a severely depressed person. I totally understood her concerns and I tried my best to reassure her that I was going to be fine. She was opposed to it but I knew it was time. I told her that I was sorry but I was going to do it and the fact that I had the six-week buffer at the end before he was born was enough security. It was enough for her to know that I could go back on them and be stable when he arrived if I needed to. I was a bit disappointed that she wasn't fully supportive but I understood her concerns. Eventually she came round to the idea, probably because she felt like she didn't have a choice.

I really liked Melbourne and would love to go back one day; it will always be the place where I felt my life took a turning point. Come to think of it, another turning point was that we didn't win any awards – our award run had come to an end, for now. It was a comedy festival, after all, and the show wasn't exactly a belly roller every second, so we knew we were just lucky to be a part of it. Some bloke in one of our shows shouted out at the start when I was still behind the curtain, something like, 'GET YOUR TITS OUT, LOVE' as Bryony introduced the show. Poor bloke thought he was walking into some-thing completely different – probably *Sex Idiot 2*. I was furious and wanted to run up the seats and tear his balls out of his bag, but the rest of the crowd made him feel like a right prick by booing and hissing him so I settled with that. At the end of the show he tried to apologise to me sarcastically and get a reaction out of me by pinching my arm. That was another personal turning point for me, as I didn't react violently. His balls stayed where they were. Other than that fool, Australia was a huge success – one that we weren't expecting at all. Our show really did just start out as a plan to spend more time with each other and anything that came after that was a bonus.

To celebrate the end of the Australian tour, Bryony and I treated ourselves to 5 nights in Sydney before flying back with our heads held high and Bryony's belly full of baby.

CHAPTER FOUR

B: So, that was Tim Grayburn. He works in adver-
tising. He is an account director at a big media
agency back in London so his days are usually spent
buying advertising space for big corporate brands [she
boos].

Or I should say that's what he used to do, up until
about six months ago when he decided to leave his
job, make this show with me and come on tour for
a year.

When we got back to the UK the reviews and media
attention we had received in Australia had
followed us home. It felt pretty cool, like we were two
victorious Olympians returning home. Although, we
didn't actually have a home to come back to because we
were on the road and it didn't make sense to pay rent
when we would hardly be there, so we used my mum
and dad's house as a base. We arrived back and arranged

for my siblings to come over to tell them the really big news. Everything was beautiful – Australia had been a success and we had a new member of the family to introduce on the back of it. Bryony had told her mum on the phone while we were in Australia but I wanted to wait to tell my lot in person. We were all sitting in the garden – Mum, Dad, Seg, Jen and Bobby – and I said, 'We've got some news.' 'YOU'RE PREGNANT?' my mum shouted. There was a big cheer and a bottle of champagne to celebrate. We couldn't have written the return home any better. It was a really lovely moment, and one where I couldn't see anything getting in the way of our future together.

There was no time to mess about, though. After only a couple of days of relaxing I went straight back to two weeks' labouring for a mate's building company. Before the news of the pregnancy I probably wouldn't have bothered but I remember feeling a sense of responsibility – I was going to be a dad and so every penny counted. I loved it – we had missed a huge chunk of the grim UK winter, it was April and I was bouncing up putting on me hard hat with the optimism that comes from having summer around the corner. While Bryony worked on another project, I was going into work with Andre every day. He's a carpenter and he worked for another mate called Goffy. Goffy was really just doing me a favour so I could earn a bit of extra cash. I wasn't qualified in building or carpentry in any way – I mostly just read

153

baby books, to be honest – so my main job was to annoy Andre by pulling down his pants in front of everyone while he tried to saw a doorframe to size. On my last day I left early to pick up Bryony and take her to the hospital for our twelve-week scan. I can't remember if I cried but I remember the incredible feeling on hearing my baby's heartbeat for the first time. It was rapid and sounded like it could have been made by a computer programme, but I knew it was his little heartbeat, like I was tuned into his channel. It was a special moment, one of many more to come.

The next morning we headed to Folkestone. There's a theatre there called Quarter House and they had agreed to let us rehearse the show there for a week and then do a one-night show for the people of Folkestone. I loved being on the move all the time but Bryony had had enough – she didn't want to live out of a bag, she wanted to nest. We had another six months to go until we would be finished or have a break from the UK tour to have the baby, though, so she just knuckled down and did what she had to do. She obviously wasn't that physically restricted at only a few months pregnant, but she felt drained and sick a lot. It was difficult because I was excited and she wasn't. She had done the touring thing before but it was my first time.

Just as we were talking about doing fewer shows so Bryony could rest more, we got a call asking us to go back to Australia for a week of shows in Brisbane. They had been offered the show before but had turned it down, thinking that it wouldn't be successful enough to fill the seats. After Perth, Adelaide and Melbourne, they wanted in, so they offered us a great package, including business class seats for Bryony (apparently I wasn't pregnant enough to get the same treatment). We needed the money so we had to agree. I tried my hardest to sneak into business class the whole way there and I got caught roughly six times and ushered back to economy. I think the longest I lasted was twenty-five minutes. It became a bit of a laugh with the staff, well for me. They probably wanted to throw me out the window. I try my luck every time I'm on a plane now. Once I managed a full twelve-hour kip on the way to Indonesia without anyone noticing, waking up and slipping back to economy before the breakfast rounds, like a sly aviator fox. I think it's a shame that we live in a world where there are plenty of empty seats in business and first class and an airline would rather no one sat in them than do a lottery for the people who can't afford to lie down on a twenty-four-hour journey they've already paid £1,000 for. It's not like they're going to sell those seats halfway over the Pacific. Anyway, aside from the air travel socialist protest, Brisbane was another sell-out and successful run – one that Bryony could really have done without. But finally it was time to go home and show them what we'd been up to Down Under.

The day after we got back from Brisbane we had our twenty-week scan. We had decided on the plane that we wanted to know if it was our little boy or girl in there.

We went to the hospital and they told us that we were going to have a little boy. I was so happy. I immediately pictured what he'd look like and imagined the day when I could kick a football around with him and have him on my shoulders. It was kind of fitting that we were having a boy, too, because of the focus of the show. We were smashing down macho masculine barriers of emotional openness and now we were creating our own little perfect version of what a man should be. The aim of the show suddenly became even more personal. We went home and relaxed for a few days to recover from the jetlag. I could tell that the news of us having a son ignited the creative engine in Bryony and the cogs began to turn; she started to think about how she could use our news in the show to drill home the message that it's important for all of us to look after our boys' mental health. We had a few days of rehearsal and then Bryony wanted to add a song and dance scene:

B&T: Quick it's a boy
Quick give that boy a truck
Quick get your boob out and give that boy a suck
[We begin to march in unison on the spot]
Quick make him tough now
Don't ever let him cry
Show him only heterosexual love
But don't tell him why
[We begin to move backwards to the mouth of the

tent]
Quick give him limits
Don't let him show his feelings
Tell him a lady's only job is staring at the ceiling
Quick show him power is only found in strength
Don't let him know that talking
Can help him see some sense
[We stop marching]
And if he's feeling sad now
Don't let him tell you so
Just say that hiding sport and beer
Is the only way to go
B: [On her own now]
Quick let him go to work now
Every single day
Even if he feels his brain is about to waste away

Bryony was constantly coming up with new scenes and it kept me on my toes. I wasn't happy that we had to learn a whole new scene just a couple of days before we were about to perform to our biggest crowd yet, in London, and with my family and friends in the audience. But I did it anyway. She was the boss and it was easier than arguing it. It was weird, even though we'd been doing the show for three months, my nerves and insecurities all came back. I had felt a bit protected in Australia because I didn't know anyone there and so I felt safe from judgement – if they didn't like the show, then who cared? But back home it was different. My family, my friends, old work colleagues, old girlfriends, they were all going to see the show and have their opinions about it. And it turned out that my WHOLE family were going to see it – Grandma, aunties, uncles, cousins – literally a busful, around thirty of them. I was really nervous before opening that night. Instead of facing a wall of strangers, I was tasked with entertaining people I knew and it would be the first time a lot of them had heard the intricacy and details of my time with depression. But I also felt that, once that show was out of the way, then nothing could stop me. That was going to be as hard as it would get. It was my grandma's birthday and she had come all the way from Morecambe to watch the show so, before the doors opened, I reserved the best seat in the house with a homemade VIP sign and put a box of chocolates on it with a card saying 'Grandma'. I was really worried about her seeing the show because she had no idea that I had ever had suicidal thoughts. I couldn't bring myself to tell her beforehand so I just mentioned that she might hear a few things that she wouldn't like and it might be upsetting. She's very tough, my grandma – she's a German woman who had been through the war – but she's very protective of her grandchildren and I wanted her to know what she was getting herself into.

After the show that night it felt like another huge weight had been lifted from my shoulders. We received a standing ovation from the 250-plus crowd and I looked into the audience and saw my whole family and my mates standing there in front of me, proud. My eyes welled up and I smiled like I'd never smiled before. No skeletons in my closet now. This is who I am, this is what happened to me, and this is how I'm dealing with it. It felt like a 'take it or leave it' moment, like I didn't have to impress anyone any more by being artificially strong or acting like nothing bothered me. I realised THIS is real strength – the strength to manage your emotions in an open and honest way is a strength that's often overlooked in men. I realised that my weakness hadn't been my depression, it had been my inability to talk about it. It's weak to be afraid of being who you really are. My weakness had actually been my FEAR of discussing or exploring my emotions. I wasn't cured there and then with this realisation, I was still under the impression that the cause of my depression was something I had no control over, something biological, some chemical unbalance. I still don't really know how much that has or had to do with my mental state. However, I was figuring out, by accident, that there are other ways to alleviate the darkness and it felt good, really good.

As we stood outside the theatre thanking everyone for coming, my mate Sam shouted, 'Well, England's lost its backbone, ain't it?' It was a hilarious moment that cleared the air and everyone hugged and it was another occasion when we were all brought together and reminded that we're only human. As I retreated to the dressing room, I realised how therapeutic the whole process had been. I guess it's similar to what it feels like to come out as being gay, in a way – just being loud and proud. You stress and worry about other people's reactions for so long and then, when you finally do it, you have a feeling of, 'Oh, no one cares. Why didn't I do this ages ago?' And, if they do care, fuck 'em. You're free to be who you want to be. Southbank was my biggest hurdle and I had survived it. I was ready to do more.

Waking up on a high the next morning, we gathered ourselves together and headed to Latitude Festival. The capacity was bigger again – this time 500. It was a music festival and I had to play and sing a song about depression in front of lots of people. I was nervous but just as excited. This was the first time I really loved performing. While I was sitting in the middle of the stage with my guitar and singing my song, I thought to myself, 'This is brilliant! What an experience. I'll never forget it.' Noel Gallagher was playing in the field next to us, probably singing 'Don't Look Back in Anger' (perhaps a theme song to our story), and I smiled as I thought that people had come to see us instead. It was the biggest crowd we had performed to so far and they were all happy festivalgoers. I felt like bloody Bono but without the shit hair and Tron sunglasses. I loved every minute of that show – it felt like every single one of us was on the same page and we got a standing ovation from the whole crowd in the big tent and it felt amazing. Rock and Roll Depression Style.

We drove back to Mum and Dad's in the countryside and decided that that was where we wanted to live when our little man entered our world. Not Mum and Dad's, but our own house in the countryside away from the hecticness of London. We agreed on a quieter life, one where we could settle down as a family. We were about to travel up to Edinburgh and spend the whole of August there and we wanted our own place to come back to. We realised that we didn't just want it, we needed it. Our son was due on 13 November and we had to have a home ready for him. Getting our own place seemed just about doable. We arranged for a few viewings and when we walked into the third viewing of the day we both knew immediately that that was going to be our nest. It was unfurnished so we were going to have to buy or source a whole houseful of stuff. It was quite stressful and we were stretched for time and money. After Edinburgh we would have two nights in Brighton and three weeks of shows at the Soho Theatre in London to go, and that would take us through to the middle of October. We would then have four weeks left to prepare for our son's arrival. After he was born we would have three months off and then go back to touring the UK when both the baby and Bryony were strong enough. It was the perfect plan. 1 September was going to be the date we got the keys to our new home. It was another one of those memorable dates – the beginning of a new time, not just because of the house but also because it would be the last day of taking medication on my current weaning plan.

It was time to travel up to the big event, Edinburgh Fringe, the biggest and best Fringe festival in the world. It spans twenty-five days of entertainment with a whopping 3,314 shows across 313 venues. We had three weeks of shows booked in at the Traverse Theatre, a small space but a well-known, highly respected theatre. I had only been to Edinburgh during the festival for a couple of days before, so it felt great to know that I was going to be part of the whole festival this time round as an artist not just a spectator. The place was buzzing. The whole city just wakes up and puts a smile on, ready to have lots of fun. I loved it. By this point we had done the show about a hundred times so it was only just becoming a bit boring for us. It felt like a job now – the best job I'd ever had, don't get me wrong – but each day I was looking forward to getting it done so I could get out there and see what the rest of the festival had to offer. Funnily enough, there were a lot of other acts that also focused on mental health. The media jumped on the mental health bandwagon and it seemed to be all over the papers and on TV. It really made it the talking point of the festival, which happily heightened the awareness of mental health in general. After a couple of days there we were asked to be interviewed as part of a three-minute report for BBC Scotland evening news; the report talked about depression as 'a major theme' of the Fringe. It promoted a 'Gala for Mental Health' hosted by the Mental Health Foundation. The Gala included us and other acts such as Le Gateau Chocolat, Carl Donnelly, Felicity Ward and Paul Merton's Impro Chums. It was a great evening and celebrated the life of Robin Williams and, in particular, the advances we were all making in tackling the taboo of mental ill-health.

The weeks that followed were much the same, a bit of a blur; it was non-stop, we were doing panel talks and were even asked to be on *Front Row* on BBC Radio 4, which was pretty cool. Following that, we went on Radio 2 and were asked to be interviewed on the TV by Gemma Cairney, which was to be aired nationally on BBC 1. We sat on a park bench in Princes Gardens, the cameras pointed at us, mic men hovering above out of shot and we talked to the country about the show. It was pretty incredible. I managed to control my nerves and speak about what we were doing with some sort of composure. The next day I received a few emails from young men and women who had seen me on TV and said that they had never heard someone talk about depression so openly and asked me to help them do the same. I replied saying that the first step was to talk to a loved one, if they hadn't already, and then take him or herself to the doctor and work out a plan to get them better. Each story was different and I was really just there for a chat, a non-judgemental fellow depressive who understood what they were going through. I wasn't qualified to talk therapy – at that time, I was still going through my own depression as well. I, too, was trying to figure it all out and get better, so I looked to them as much as they did me. I didn't have the answers to my own problems yet.

Towards the back end of the festival my composure and happiness started to take a bit of a wobble. I was fine and coping but the dose of citalopram in my system was becoming so low that it might as well not have been in there. It felt like a wave of panic in my body – an engine room running out of coal, knowing that the ship still had 200 miles to go. I felt sick, I had constant headaches and my sleep started to become disrupted again. My energy levels were low and I could feel it happening again. I was slowly slipping down the bank, headed for a depression pit. I wasn't sad but I knew I was getting that way.

One night at 4:30am, as I tried to get to sleep, I could hear the words 'a song came whistling through the woods' over and over again in my head. It was one of Bryony's songs that she sang as a vocal warm up before showtime. I could feel my brain going on fast forward – certain songs repeated over and over and over again in my head. It happened to me a lot and it still does. But it could be anything, it doesn't have to be a song – it can be something someone has said passing in the street, one particular lyric from a song or a quote from a film I watched five years ago. It drives me mental and keeps me up. It's the beginning of the darkness creeping back in and cloaking all the happiness. I start to think about things, a lot of things. I start to hate myself, doubt myself, worry about communicating anything to anyone and I do this until it's time to get up. Why? I have no reason to think like that – my life couldn't be any better and I should be sleeping like a log and bouncing up with enthusiasm. Then somewhere during the day I realise that it's because I have clinical depression. One man asked this question in a post-show discussion: 'Everyone has bad days – what's the difference with depression?' It's a fair question. Not many people do know the difference, and it's not taught or discussed enough for people who don't suffer to understand. A simple answer is, it's a prolonged bad day for a week, two weeks, a month. An easier way to understand it is this – it's not just a bad day because you car won't start or your boss is being a wanker, or even because you're fed up with the world. It's an uninvited, uncontrollable sadness – not anger or fed-upness – real sadness, sadness you feel when you break up with someone, lose someone, or your dog dies. What adds to this sadness is the confusion – why? You haven't broken up with someone, or lost someone and you don't even have a dog. So why are you feeling this?

I remembered the intensity of that feeling when it first happened to me when I was twenty-five and I prayed it wouldn't come back.

However, there was one difference this time – I did believe it was going to be temporary and I felt that I was prepared for it. It was the physical symptoms that were bothering me more than anything – my head hurt, my eyes looked caved in, it was like I'd been vacuum-packed from the inside, sucking my soul into a resealable bag that I could have back once depression was done with it. I'd read, though, that you need to treat the withdrawal period like a drug addict would, or any addict for that matter. You'll hurt for a while but when it's completely out of your system you'll start to regenerate and balance. I had never got past the bad part, had never managed to regenerate and balance – the withdrawal had always been too hard or life was too busy to be able to sit it out. I still had the drug in my system – I had a couple of weeks to go until I would move into our new house and life would be less full on, then I could go into regeneration mode.

We did twenty-two shows at the Traverse Theatre and sold out every single one. It was so popular that every date was sold out before the first week of the festival had even finished. It was handy because it took a lot of pressure off. It was a luxury that not a lot of acts have because of the sheer amount of competition. After speaking to a few people I found out that having to sell their shows on the streets is the bugbear of the whole festival for them. Thankfully we didn't have to do that. I would have felt a little uncomfortable selling a show about me to strangers. Although, they weren't all strangers, as I found out. Laura, my first proper girlfriend from ten years earlier, popped up in my inbox with an email saying she had come to watch the show and snuck out when I wasn't looking because she thought it would be 'weird'. Yeah, pretty weird; imagine if halfway through the show I had caught a glimpse of her illuminated in the audience like some sort of scarecrow; I would have shit myself. It turned out she had a story she wanted to share with me about depression – it wasn't her own, but still, it's another example of how depression is universal, it swirls around all of us, the ones lucky enough to escape it will more than likely be close to someone who hasn't.

One day when we were on our way into the theatre, we noticed a huge queue outside the box office and when we got inside I asked what they were there for – we had already sold out. They told me that the people outside were queuing in case anyone didn't turn up for their tickets! It was all quite overwhelming but exciting, knowing that we were gathering up such a storm and people really wanted to see the show. Bryony's agent Cath decided that we should try and capitalise on this interest and see if we could book a final one-off big gig. There was talk of the Assembly Hall, which is a beautiful venue atop The Mound and is the most prestigious venue of the Fringe. This was a huge venue that had a capacity of 650 people. It was the biggest theatre I'd ever seen. I thought, 'Surely we can't sell this out! Our little show, made by the two of us in our living room?' We high-fived when we got the news that it was going ahead – there was to be one extra show at the end of the festival for all the people who couldn't get a ticket, like a festival wrap up. Again, it sold out and we couldn't quite believe it. We got to work and rehearsed in the space and made it look and feel the best we could. It did feel right; it felt like the perfect place to top off our festival. The night went perfectly and Bryony and I didn't put a foot wrong; it was our BIG gig and we nailed it. At the end, I looked up and all 650 people were on their feet clapping. Bryony looked at me and we both cuddled and cried with happiness. The day before we left Edinburgh we were told that we had won a Herald Angel Award for Best Theatre. We were over the moon. It had been an incredible festival. Now, with our bags packed, we could retreat back to the countryside. Perfect.

My last day of taking medication was Tuesday 1 September 2015, the day we got the keys to our new house. By Friday I called Dr Scott; the first person who had diagnosed me all those years ago. I told her that I was struggling and I didn't feel well. It's hard to put into words exactly how I did feel; it's even harder to try and remember how I felt because I didn't even know at the time. I just knew I wasn't feeling right; I was very sad. She was really nice and presented me with the option of calling 'Healthy Minds' – a service provided for anyone aged eighteen or older, where you can refer yourself to have psychological therapy, mainly CBT. I think she knew how determined I was to see this withdrawal period out, so she refrained from suggesting I go back on the medication. I said it was early days but that I'd call 'Healthy Minds' if it got worse. Through the haze I somehow realised that I wasn't exactly thinking straight and might not know if it got worse (from my own experience, after an extended period of being depressed it is hard to gauge what level of sadness you feel day to day), so I decided it was time to write in the old 'D Diary' again:

D Diary
W/C 31ˢᵗ August – Finished medication on the 1st
Sept.Wobbly week, very angry and disturbed sleep
W/C 7th September – Fatigued and very tired
W/C 14th September – Starting to feel better. Had
2 great days of clear head then foggy and tired. Diet
has been good. Taken ginkgo leaf every day

I can remember the difference I felt when I had those '2 great days of clear head'. It was as if my head literally cleared the clouds and I could see what real life was like. And then someone shouted 'That's enough' and pulled me back down into the grey rainstorm. I remember crying and just wanting for it not to be me any more. I didn't want to be up and down all the time, I wanted to be above the clouds always, not just for a couple of days. I know I sound melodramatic and I can see why people who have never experienced clinical depression think it's self-centred and over the top and that there are people with much more suffering. There are, I know that now and I knew that then, but when you're in it, it really is that dramatic. You really are so consumed with how you feel because it's a priority not to keep slipping further and further away from reality.

Unfortunately on one of the not-so-clear days we had a big BBC crew come up from London to interview me and Bryony for an episode of *Arts Night* on BBC 2. We sat in the garden and spoke about how art can ease the symptoms of depression and it was cool. We filmed in my mum and dad's garden, as it was bigger and nicer than ours. The cameras were filming with the house behind us. It cracked me up, my parents were so excited to have a TV crew in their garden; my mum made everyone tea and Dad was pottering around in the background trying to get in shot like those people you see on the news. I think it's the only time in my life I've seen him clean the windows! It was another nice experience and we gave a good interview but really I was struggling inside.

I decided to call 'Healthy Minds'. The eligibility

process was a questionnaire, like my original HADS form, that took place over the phone with answers such as: Not at all; Several days; More than half the week; Nearly everyday. I'm no scientist but surely several days can easily be mixed up with nearly every day? I just had this sense that it wasn't what I needed. It seemed so impersonal, so loose. 'Healthy Minds' is a nice idea but unfortunately it has many flaws and, more than likely, that's down to a lack of funding. There are only limited spaces and what's on offer is usually a group therapy session where one's real problems are never looked at in the detail they deserve. However, I was clutching at straws, I was trying to get as much back-up as possible to keep the weaning plan alive so I persisted. I wanted as many resources as possible to be there in case I fell hard. At the end of the call I was told that I should get a letter in one week confirming an imminent appointment. Two weeks went by and I didn't receive any letter. I called back and was told that there had been an admin error and that I had 'slipped through the net'! The next available appointment was now 29 December. I couldn't believe it. 'Slipped through the net.' This ain't no fishing trip, love, this is my life. What if I were suicidal? People's lives can't be treated in this nonchalant way by the health system we are supposed to trust.

I turned to researching herbal remedies that claimed to help. Ginkgo Biloba is a supplement that apparently supports mental function and can help with mild cases of depression. I saw it in Holland and Barrett once and thought I'd give it a go. I took it every day for a week and it didn't work; for me it was like trying to knock a brick wall down with a feather. It may help others, it may help me another time in my life, but it didn't at that particular time.

On 19 September we packed up a big bag once again and went back to London to stay in a flat in Soho while we did our four-week run at the Soho Theatre. This was our last stint before we could take our well-earned break, have a baby, and enjoy him with no distractions for three months. I wasn't doing well and I felt pretty terrible.

W/C 21st September – Feel pretty awful. Mentally fine, quite frantic. Physically – sick, heavy eyes, very tired, vivid dreams still, took 2 5-HTPs Monday and Tuesday. Going to stop until the 6 weeks are up. No dairy for diet. Feel ill, swollen glands and bad headaches

I had a slight clearing of my depression but my main focus was how bad I was feeling physically. I wasn't sleeping well and felt weak. I went back to Holland and Barrett as soon as we got to London and bought some 5-HTP – another herbal medicine that claims to help with symptoms of depression and anxiety, including insomnia, by increasing the production of serotonin. According to my diary, I must have decided that I only wanted to take them when I had made it through the 6-week withdrawal period. It must have been so I could really see if they had an effect on my system that was free of any medication or chemicals. I wanted a clean slate. I had also read somewhere that it could be eating dairy that was making me tired and lethargic, so I decided to give that up. I cut it out of my diet and I think it helped, slightly. It picked up my energy by about 1–2 per cent – any improvement was welcome at that point. I was experimenting with anything and everything I had read about that might make me feel better.

We got through the first week of shows, Bryony was tired and heavily pregnant, and I was shoving myself full of herbal tablets. We stayed professional and did the show every night to the best of our ability. It had become a bit like riding a bike and it didn't take that much energy to get through the hour. Bryony and I were bickering quite a bit because neither of us wanted to be there and, at the same time, we kind of felt guilty that we were so lucky to be doing what we were doing and yet we weren't massively enjoying ourselves. Our heads were in the cottage back in Oxford and we just wanted to meet the baby. After the shows we'd have a soft drink in the bar, chat to a few people, and then head home to eat and watch a film together. We were on countdown and we just had to stick in there.

W/C 28th September – Have some virus so energy is

still low. Wednesday – woke up late 10:30am, felt in a very bad mood all day, hated the world and felt lost. Thursday – didn't sleep very well last night but feel in a better mood

I remember walking around Soho with a huge chip on my shoulder that Wednesday. I had to go and buy a few things for the new house and I found being in the shops really stressful. I couldn't function properly; I couldn't organise myself to get from one place to another with ease. It reminded me of the bus episode when I had felt out of control but this time I was angry, too. The anger came from one tiny little episode in Pret where a complete prick jumped the queue of ten people or so and asked to pay for his juice. The person behind the till didn't say anything and neither did the customer at the front of the queue so I said, 'Excuse me, mate, there's a queue here.' He turned around and looked at me from my feet to my eyes and said, 'I'm busy, mate, fuck off.' That one little glimpse of bad human behaviour spiralled my mind out of control to thinking that all humans were bad. I started to think, 'What have we done? Look how we're living our lives, this can't be it?' Before I knew it I hated my existence and hated the world. I felt completely lost. I had no direction and I couldn't see past the next ten minutes. If I'd been feeling healthy, I would have just laughed at that bloke and said something to embarrass him to get my revenge but instead I felt like Michael

Douglas in *Falling Down* and I wanted to stick a shotgun up his arse and pull the trigger. I remember coming home and telling Bryony about it and she said that that sort of thing was happening to me a lot lately. It made me think that the guy had been put there to test me. It made me think, was it me, not him? The guy was a twat, but it's how I reacted to it that made it my problem. I couldn't let it go. I think I was just hyper sensitive. Sensitive or not, though, I knew my anger was becoming a problem and I didn't want to end up scrapping again.

W/C 5th October – *Very angry, very intolerant, hate the world*

It didn't get any better. I didn't want to be around anyone other than Bryony. By the end of the week even she was annoying me. I was beginning to shut myself off from the world again. I'm pretty sure that if Maisy had been around I would have started the lonely walks to the treehouse tree again. I tried to think differently but I couldn't. I tried to see the good in people rather than the bad; but every thought was negative or pessimistic and I couldn't turn it around. I just woke up and did what ever Bryony told me to do; I wasn't capable of making plans.

On 7 October, Bryony told me we had a meeting with the publishing company Hodder and Stoughton. They wanted to know if we were interested in writing a book about our story. It was another exciting, amazing piece of news for us but I couldn't muster up more than a smile about it. I was beginning to lose hope that I would ever get better.

W/C 12ᵗʰ October – Feel better. Still frantic and anxious. Can't calm my brain. Still feel rough when I wake up. Started 5-HTP

We had one more week of shows to go. I started to feel a little better, probably because I could see the finish line and I knew it was finally going to be just Bryony and me in the peace and quiet. I started to take the 5-HTP and didn't see any difference but I took them anyway. Then I started to wake up feeling hungover, like I had drunk a bottle of vodka and smoked forty fags. I wasn't drinking so I thought it must be my body crying out for the chemicals it had been so used to. I started to get brain zaps as well. Brain zaps are just that – out of nowhere it feels like Zeus is firing a bolt of lightning through your nut. It's not a nice feeling, as you can imagine. I also threw up. I googled these symptoms and discovered that I was going through 'Antidepressant discontinuation syndrome' and it was quite normal to experience all of this, especially since I had been on medication for such a long period of time.

I was a mess during that last week and was still performing every night. Bryony was so tired and only four weeks away from her due date and yet she was still performing every night, too. We were running out of steam but we could see the end. We were broken but that made each performance so raw and real that I think they were some of our best shows. We had sold out every night, once again, and we had a few standing ovations here and there; it felt like we had really connected to the audience. We were telling the truth, too, and added into the show that I was off my tablets and we gave a update every night of how it was going. I cried on stage when I talked about my unborn son and my worries that he may, too, have to go through all of this. The response from the audience was full of hope and we finished the first leg of our UK tour with a positive, hopeful outlook towards the future.

We finally got home to our cottage and I experienced another huge turning point in my life. I told Bryony that I was feeling very emotional, I felt like I was about to cry every second of the day. She told me to go and lie down, so I went up to the baby's room that was all ready and waiting for him. I sat on the bed and I cried and cried. For the first time in my life I was crying controllably. I knew it was something that I needed to do to feel better and, instead of locking it inside to fester, along with my outdated opinion that crying makes me weak, I just let it rip. I knew I was happy – we had finished a tour of our really successful theatre show, we had our new house and we were only three weeks away from our baby boy joining us. I knew I was happy. I took a picture of myself crying and smiling at the same time to remember that the tears weren't a reflection of how I was feeling. For me, this unlocked an ancient secret, hidden deep down inside myself. I finally understood that I could be happy in a general sense and sad at the same time if I needed to be. It didn't have to be just one or the other. Some days I will feel emotional and some days I won't. That's life; that's my life. All I can do is take very good care of myself and enjoy the wonders that creep up on me, good or bad. I knew that I was going to do it this time – that episode of crying was a victory cry, a happy cry, a positive optimistic cry towards my future with my wife and son. One day I may get depressed again, one day I may get cancer, one day I might grow a fourth leg. My future is unwritten and I realised that I can't control it, I just have to enjoy it the very best I can. I wiped my tears and went downstairs, I found Bryony in the living room and I put my arms around her and our unborn baby and smiled in silence. Since that moment I've never had to write in the D Diary again.

PART III

CHAPTER ONE

Before Frank was born I was 95 per cent better. Without doubt the show and the whole experience of 'coming out' got me to the finish line, but Frank's arrival pushed me across that ribbon and straight into the next race. He arrived on 8 November 2015 at 12:01pm. Remembrance Sunday – certainly won't forget that one. We named him Frank after the granddad I had only met as a baby myself. He had a full head of hair and a beautiful yet gremlin-looking sort of face. I'm going to say it; it was the happiest moment of my life. He was here, he was healthy and we were a family, something I'd looked forward to since I was a young man. I'm not going to go into detail about how much he means to me because that's something for me and him to talk about one day, but you get the picture. Life was truly beautiful and I could see it clearly. He immediately made me a better person. I had to be better, not only for him but also for myself. I will always be indebted to my boy for that and I can't wait to learn more from him, as we grow older together.

Your children are not your children.
They are the sons and daughters of Life's longing for
*   itself.*
They come through you but not from you,
And though they are with you yet they belong not to
*   you.*

You may give them your love but not your thoughts,
For they have their own thoughts.
You may house their bodies but not their souls,
For their souls dwell in the house of tomorrow,
which you cannot visit, not even in your dreams.
You may strive to be like them,
but seek not to make them like you.
For life goes not backward nor tarries with yesterday.

You are the bows from which your children
as living arrows are sent forth.
The archer sees the mark upon the path of the infinite,
and He bends you with His might
that His arrows may go swift and far.
Let your bending in the archer's hand be for gladness;
For even as He loves the arrow that flies,
so He loves also the bow that is stable.

I've been reading a book called *The Road Less Travelled* by M. Scott Peck and a recurrent theme of the book is the importance of 'spiritual growth' in yourself and your children. It's where I found the above poem by Kahlil Gibran on what it should be to raise a child. Oddly Bryony's mum also sent it to us just before Frank was born. The book's a great read, by the way, one that was recommended to me by someone who came to see the show in Melbourne. He was a really troubled bloke who had seen and been involved in a lot of bad things during his life; you could see in his eyes that he had experienced real emotional pain for a long time and he told me that he had worked very hard to get to a stable place in his life and that *The Road Less Travelled* had been a vital tool in helping him get there. I've only just got round to reading it and I have found that a lot of it relates to my life right now and therefore really stands out as an aid to making myself a better person and keeping me stable. I guess when you're ill, knowledge and literature and the experience of others who have been there before is vital for getting better. I have found that reading whatever I can get my hands on to improve myself has helped me enormously. Reading about positive methods and ways to live your life, while being good to others is key. It distracts you from your ego. Learning about us humans, as one, rather than as individuals fighting it out for money, status and power, allows our souls to shine through. I've learnt that our egos and souls are constantly battling it out and that the ego acts as an attention-seeking bully who suffocates the soul. When my obsession with money, success and finding out where my ego fits into the world disappeared, my soul was able to come to the surface and I found out how good that felt. It felt natural and real and light. Of course, the ego will always be there and unfortunately most people in today's society direct more of their attention to keeping their ego happy rather than the soul. As I am starting to realise, switch it around and you'll start to feel better – don't care so much about that new TV and care more about how you communicate with a loved one or care about the human race as a whole and you will start to feel and see life differently.

There is a reason why people say that helping others helps you. It is the work of the soul. It can be on any level, you don't have to jack your job in, just helping an old person with their shopping bags or standing back and letting someone get on the tube before you will make you feel better, I promise. For me, the idea that our show was helping others in turn helped me.

Reading about mental health and trying to understand it has probably helped me more than anything else. And it's not just reading about mental health, it's reading about anything, anything that interests me. Find a will-ingness to seek new information and change things. I was lucky and managed to identify a trigger for my depres-sion and that was my obsession with the 'purpose of life' and trying to understand where and how the universe started. Then one day I started to read about philosophy and to watch science documentaries about cosmology. It's so important to identify what's wrong and then put your energy into discovering what will help. For me, books do this. I look at them as a private one-on-one teacher or a free therapist. You learn while sitting in silence or lying on your back and zoning into a literary world that ignores the frantic world around you. It's like a form of meditation and I believe it soothes the soul without you even knowing it.

I think it's unlikely that we wake up one day and just find ourselves depressed. It probably happens over a period of time, as a series of reactions to difficult situations and negative thinking. I believe depression is a rational response to a bad situation that you need to address: maybe you hate your job, you've lost someone or your relationship is not working, for example. I couldn't figure out what I needed to change for a very long time so I'm not saying that it's easy to identify. But you have to put more effort than I did into finding out what is wrong. Too many people, including me, don't address those niggling issues, whatever they may be. You have to find that willingness to do it from somewhere in order to change your life. Would we rather blame our depression on a chemical imbalance or the stresses of everyday life? It certainly seems less daunting to blame an imbalance, rather than jacking in that job or ending that relationship? In some cases, I think we do. We look at depression as the problem when I believe we should recognise it as a helpful symptom that alerts us to the fact that something needs to change. We shouldn't ask ourselves what is wrong with us; we should ask ourselves what happened to us? We should do this by rationally breaking down how we behave, how we react and how we reflect. When I started to look at what happened in my life to make me depressed, rather than just concede to the fact that I was broken and couldn't be fixed, I started to mend. If you have been diagnosed with depression you are classed as mentally unwell. I think the opposite is true. If you have depression, you are responding to a negative situation. Surely this proves you are mentally healthy. It means you are in tune with what is happening in your life; chose to see your depression as a beacon through the fog of life. You are exercising a way of fixing something that is fundamentally wrong in your life. You're exploring and questioning your existence. That's not being mentally unwell, that's progressive. Depression is merely a symptom of a curious, challenging mind and you need to take notice of it as soon as possible before the fog becomes too thick.

If you do fall into depression, strip away all things that are unimportant. Make choices in the moment as well as for the future. Separate what has meaning from what is essentially meaningless. Realise how beautiful life is – real life, that is, not just a Facebook life. Real life is fresh air, a simple meal, free walks in the park. We have disconnected with real life too much and, personally, when I quit Facebook, Instagram and all other forms of social media that I had found myself using to waste time and which generated an anxiety about how my profile should look to the outside world, it really helped me. I'm not going to give it a total bashing because I do think it's good for business and raising awareness about important issues, but it's also a platform for bullying and idleness. It has created a new splurge of anxiety in the world where people structure their profile to make their life seem amazing to others, instead of stepping back and asking themselves if they are really happy. Life is a series of moments, perceptions and choices but, above all, it is painfully short – why spend it looking at what someone else is doing? Focus on your own life and the people you love and the people in the world who need your attention – not your old school friend who has bought a new Land Rover and plastered it all over Instagram. Life should be lived to the fullest; the present moment is everything. We need to remind ourselves of this.

I look back at stuff I've written in this book and I'm not happy with it but that has been my problem throughout my life – I'm constantly trying to rewrite my past when really I should be writing my future and focusing on the now. Limit your time in the parallel universe of Facebook – it isn't the future. It isn't real. More often than not, it's a dishonest reflection of the past. Look at your past to learn from it, not change it. For example, you can look at who has been important to you in your past and who hasn't. You can use it as an exercise in identifying the people who haven't been nice to you and have no concern for your growth and so pick out the people who are important to you, people that you want to grow with. I've become quite ruthless and if I think someone is negative and nasty and selfish, then I don't exhaust myself by giving him or her time, time that I could spend with someone who is nice and may need it and give back what I put in. I've learnt not to react and let nastiness affect me as much as it once did. Fighting fire with fire doesn't work. Just walk away. Don't get embroiled in someone else's negative ways. It is hard to do but I'm learning. It happened to me recently and it ruined my whole morning – someone was not very nice and my anxiety about the situation was hard to settle. But it did eventually and I was allowed to continue the rest of my day as if nothing had happened and I continued on my positive path. If I had reacted to the situation with anger and negativity, which is how I would have done once, then the problem would have spilled into the next day and so on. Basically, let horrible people be horrible on their own. Avoid people who aren't interested in helping you make yourself a better person.

This year I've found out about the death of three people I knew. They were all men aged under thirty-six. Two were accidents, one was believed to be suicide. Each time I heard the news I was shocked, saddened and then I came to the realisation that death is inevitable however it happens. It sounds obvious, I know, but we live our life on the edge of immortality; we forget that it can be over any second of any day. We're brought up with the idea that when we die it'll be in bed in our favourite pjs, the sun going down at the same rate as our eyes lids close, drifting off into a world of fluffy bunny rabbits and weightlessness. As I get older, I try to remember that only the lucky ones get that lotto ticket. But also, it doesn't matter if that's the way you go or not. Of course it matters how you go to your loved ones, but it doesn't to you, you will have passed through. To you the only thing that matters is all the stuff leading up to the credits rolling. Reminding yourself of this daily can help you enjoy the film of life, even when it gets boring, sad or just plain rubbish. You can never question the decision that someone takes to end their own life because you can't possibly know how they feel. However, I would urge anyone contemplating it, not to go through with it, even if you have to say to yourself that you're just delaying it because it's a new day tomorrow. Quite possibly the new day will still be a shit one, possibly even worse, but there will be better ones ahead, I can promise you that. Most importantly, though, there will be a younger you out there who needs your experience to learn from and will need you to help them spiritually grow.

I think one of the worst things for depression is worrying about it. Worrying about what it is, blaming yourself for feeling that low, spending the little energy you have pretending that you're not low in front of people and, above all, the sheer lack of understanding about what is happening to you. Why aren't I sleeping? Why do I feel sick when I'm not sick (physically)? Why am I crying? It's all so new and fucking scary that you get lost in it. I'm in no way saying it's as easy as reading a book to cure it but, for me, an overall understanding of what depression is and what it means for me personally has helped me begin to conquer it. Pick up a book and force yourself to read.

Being honest allows you to flow through life. It causes less stress and helps you live freely. For me I had a deep sadness about not being able to be proud of who I was. I was ashamed. I couldn't see the positives of my diagnosis so I pretended to be someone else. That dishonesty, not only to myself but also the people around me, slowly made me worse. I figured out what I needed to do to be saved and that was to live honestly. I realized that speaking falsely only adds to the confusion of the world and there's enough of that as there is! The truth shall set you free, believe me. I remember thinking about why most of us automatically answer 'good' whenever anyone asks us how we are. Even if we're not good, we say we are. Why? Is it because we don't want to burden people with our problems or we have to uphold the default social status of being happy? Probably a bit of both. Once when someone asked me at a party how I felt I decided to be completely honest. This person was a stranger, he looked like a nice bloke so I said, 'Not good; I'm depressed and my anxiety is through the roof right now.' He happened to be a meditation expert and he taught me some methods to deal with my anxiety in social situations. We ended up talking for about an hour and a half and I left that party feeling much better than when I went in. If I had lied and said I was 'good', there may have been nowhere for that conversation to go or, at least, it would have been an on-the-surface bullshit chitchat with nothing gained. And, thinking about it, he might very well have gained something from helping me, too – win, win.

To be more honest you need confidence. Confidence is something I was lacking and something that Bryony gave me. She encouraged me not to be afraid of voicing my opinion. I had never learned to look to myself for an opinion on how I should live my life. I monitored the emotions of others around me to see how I was doing. If people thought that I was doing well and they thought that I was happy then I believed it, without actually asking myself if I was. There's a big difference between genuine confidence and ballsy, cocky, fake confidence, which I used to have. People associate confidence with arrogance. What we really associate with arrogance is that fake mask of confidence. It is arrogant because it's not real. Confidence doesn't have to be arrogant, it doesn't need to be shouted from the rooftops; it is something you should feel. Confidence in your identity, confidence in wanting to live, confidence in love and confidence in accepting who you are – these are attributes we should all strive to have.

Keeping busy also really helps. It's a bit of vicious cycle when you're depressed, though, because it's hard to find the energy, or the care, to keep busy. And if you overdo it and don't rest, then you can push yourself further into depression. It's a fine balance. Over the past couple of days I've rekindled my friendship with Stav. It's been about 3 years since we've really hung out properly and the love is still there but we've also got a new thing in common, which makes the friendship stronger than it ever was. We've both been on what seem to be identical paths of self-discovery. What did it? A wedding (that I almost didn't go to). All it took was an opportunity to spend more than 5 minutes together. It's so important to see people, do things, volunteer, run, go to a free seminar on something completely random, start a cooking course or travel – I could go on and on, but ultimately just getting up and moving opens the door to potential happiness. One day the door might be a rubbish one and fuck all is behind it, but you'll never know until you open it. Ever since the very first Nike slogan was aired on TV, my old man has always said 'JUST DO IT'. The old bugger was right. But there is a catch, I'm not currently clinically depressed and everything I've just written makes total sense to me. It puts a smile on my face and I feel happiness in discovery. However, when I was depressed 'JUST DO IT' seemed like the most complicated algorithm of all time. There were no doors, just brick walls. That's why I think it's so important never to assume someone can just start doing things. If they don't, it means they can't. It means they need help to get to the point where they can. And I don't mean help in getting dressed and being pushed out into the world, I mean they need to start at the very beginning and formulate a long, slow plan to kill off the main chunk of depression in order to be able to start loving and exploring life.

The fatigue that depression brings not only makes it hard personally but it also has a huge impact on our global productivity and economic growth. I went to a talk before we started to make the show that had been put on by *The Economist* and Kofi Annan was the guest speaker, along with loads of other important, intelligent people all with a passion for discussing the 'Global Crisis of Depression'. There were politicians from all over Europe, neuroscientists, physiologists, charities and the World Health Organisation. It was pretty fascinating and there were two main issues that stood out for me – the importance of education and awareness of mental illnesses at a grass roots level, and addressing the lack of political will when it comes to fixing the problem. We have the resources but we aren't doing enough to prevent, discuss or treat mental illness. If I had been able to sit in on that talk before I got depression, maybe I would have learnt how to avoid it by using the knowledge I gained about what it is, who it affects and how it can be treated. Norman Lamb MP stood up and talked openly about his experience with depression. Someone in the audience thanked him for his bravery. He replied, 'That's very kind but it's not bravery, it's just being honest.' For me, that was a big, fat, middle finger to the stigma surrounding depression. If there is a stigma surrounding something, then it is brave to talk about it openly but saying so lets the stigma win. It confirms that the stigma is real. By saying that he wasn't being brave, old Norm was saying to everyone that he was standing up to the stigma of depression by being honest. I loved it and used it throughout the tour and continue to use it in everyday life. Whenever anyone says I am brave for standing up and speaking about my depression, I use Norman's line, even though I really want to say, 'Yeah, I know, I'm the bravest, ain't I?' The point is, people like Norman made people like me begin to be more honest. It is a simple life lesson for all kids and young adults to learn, surely?

I seek all this information out about the world of mental illness now that I've gone through it and made it out the other side, but how much better would it have been if I had been able to learn about the dangers and reality of it before experiencing it? We're shielded from too much of what makes us adult – I'm not saying we should take people's childhoods away by making them privy to the horrors of real life, but at least tee them up so it's not such a shock when bad things happen. More needs to be done in schools to teach children about real life. I don't just mean about how to get a good job – teenagers and even children can be diagnosed with depression and anxiety, so why are they not being made aware of it in schools? I'd like to think that nowadays they are but I certainly wasn't. The leading cause of death for people between the ages of ten and nineteen is suicide. We can't have people of that age taking their own lives; it has to stop. Sick beds were the only things I remember about being ill at school. If you felt physically ill, like a tummy bug or a cold, you would be sent to see the school nurse. We didn't know what anxiety was back then. I really believe that depression and anxiety should be added to the criteria of illnesses that allow you to go and see the school nurse. And the nurse should be trained in how to deal with a depressive episode, a panic attack or complete mental breakdown. I believe the education system is failing in many ways and I wouldn't be surprised if the 'survival of the fittest' attitude in schools has a lot to do with the psychological structuring of young minds. Merit shouldn't be given just to whether you're good at maths, we should be trying to help children become decent members of society who understand that compassion and sharing is just as important as being able to solve a few equations.

I also feel we've been let down by the government and the health system. I am hugely grateful for everything the NHS has done for me and my family, but it has its flaws when it comes to mental health. I question whether I needed to be on tablets for seven years. Could I have been cured with therapy? We'll never know, but I'd like to think so. It's nuts to think that literally anyone can get their hands on powerful, mind-altering drugs by ticking a few boxes. It's as easy as convincing your mum you have a cold and can't go to school by shutting off your airway and talking in a funny voice. I was left to my own devices – left to continue repeating my prescription and keeping quiet. There was no plan or desire to find out where the problem lay. It feels like 'they' were just happy that I was feeding the pharmaceutical giant and not being a nuisance with frequent doctor appointments. I really do believe that if more money were directed into therapy rather than medication we would see vast improvements in the health and happiness of society. But, of course, it's something that would take time and we humans like quick fixes; we love our plasters. If I had been prescribed a course of therapy sessions as a young man when it all first started, I think I would have figured a lot of shit out then and avoided seven years of confusion and struggle.

Like any industry, there are doubts and conspiracy theories about practices in psychiatry. There's a worrying link between the people who write the rulebooks on diagnoses and the people who sell the drugs; like lobbyists funding presidential marketing campaigns in exchange for laws that make their clients more money. This obviously brings up concerns about the increasing tendency to write prescriptions for patients who may not show patterns of behaviour extreme enough to be taking those drugs. It's worrying to think that the casual diagnoses and prescriptions that happen could be for the benefit of pharmaceutical companies and not the patient themselves, but in today's world it doesn't seem so far-fetched. I do feel for the incredibly intelligent scientists and doctors, though, who have so many variables to consider when it comes to psychiatric illness. They are doing all the hard work and then having to justify their results to the people with the power and money – often having their research rubbished because of some other political pressure. Health should never be sacrificed for economic or financial reasons.

Without a doubt changing my diet has also helped my depression. I was never a bad eater but I had no real regard for what I shoved in my stomach; I would gorge on anything that tasted good without understanding what it was actually doing in there. I have since realised that the mind and body are in tune with one another and when one isn't well, the other isn't either. I tried a few things and some of them worked and some didn't. Over the last three years it's been trial and error but now I think I've got the right balance. First to go was caffeine.

I used to love coffee – I loved the smell, the taste and the kick it gave me and, if I'm being honest, it was a bit like smoking – I thought it was pretty cool ('pretty cool' to pay £4 for an espresso then knock it back with a rolled up newspaper under your arm). However, when my anxiety got to the point where I wasn't in control, I was drinking three cups of coffee a day – not crazy but enough to rattle the cage. Surely that wouldn't help a fragile mind, I thought, so I stopped. It was my first step in giving up something that I enjoyed for the greater good of my mind. I haven't drunk caffeine regularly for three years now and not only do I feel good because I don't have the drug running through my neurological path-ways, I feel good because I've been able to stick to something I said I was going to do to help me. I have, without a doubt, identified one trigger and managed to cross it off the list. I drink all sorts of herbal teas nowadays – they're cleaner, purer and seem to heal the mind instead of sending it bouncing off the walls of my skull. Every now and then, maybe once every three months, *if* I'm feeling as though I can handle it, I'll have a coffee. Rock and roll man.

Here are a few other dos and don'ts in the world of culinary depression. You've heard of the D Diary, this is my D Diet:

Water – Drink lots of it. It's the soul's engine oil.
Cow's milk – Don't drink lots of it. It's for baby cows.

Vegetables – Learn how to cook with them; they're as natural as the sky and should be eaten.

Factory foods – Avoid them; they're as natural as Donald Trump's soul.

Pulses – Beans, lentils and peas give you energy and everything you need and are cheaper and better for the environment than the water-pumped meat our supermarkets sell nowadays.

Fizzy drinks – Cut out this devil's piss, that amount of sugar is not needed.

Three meals a day – No matter how depressed you are, force yourself to eat. You've got enough on your plate without worrying about nutrition. No pun intended.

Alcohol – Enjoy it; don't abuse or lean on it.

Lemon, Ginger and Honey Tea – I think it helps me; it clears my head first thing in the morning.

Fruit – Glorious fruit! You don't have to eat five a day, just make sure you get enough throughout the week. Substitute that packet of crisps or Lion bar (I love a Lion bar) with a piece of fruit.

Lion bar – You have to enjoy yourself now and again as a reward for all the good behaviour.

I could go on and on but I think you get the point – it's about balance. For me, a general overhaul of my eating and drinking habits gave me more energy to bounce up and continue to live a healthier life. I wanted to know that whatever it was that was going on inside my brain had the support of what was going on inside my body. I know it's hard and expensive to eat well but eventually I realized it was more important to spend money on good food than to spend money on good beer. I think it's ridiculous that natural, healthy food is more expensive than the frozen shit you get – it's not right. We should all have the option to eat well, no matter how much we earn. Having said that, eating badly is also a result of laziness not just wealth. Either way, think about how you feel when you've overindulged; it doesn't feel good, does it? Learn to live a balanced life when it comes to food and drink. If, like me, you find it makes a difference, you'll never go back to being a greedy bastard.

Exercise is also key to keeping a healthy mind. It's no secret that sexy little endorphins are released when we exercise and make us feel good, happy and positive. I know it's frustrating that you have to sweat your balls or breasts off to get them but nothing's for free, and the feeling is worth the hard work. It is hard to get yourself motivated, even if you don't suffer from depression, but having depression is like doing the exercise with a 200kg body suit on. When you're depressed, you don't care about anything at all, so why would you care about how tight your tush is? However, every exercise session is a small win in building your brain back up from the ruins that it's in and, before you know it, you're hooked and the energy you put into drinking or shopping is directed into keeping fit. A few workouts won't cure depression but it's one of a number of things that will work together to alleviate the symptoms.

There's the saying 'Just say yes', implying that you should jump at every opportunity; much like what I was saying about 'JUST DO IT'. However, there is a difference – 'JUST DO IT' is meant to encourage you to do the thing that you've been indecisive about for a long time: that uni course, joining a football team, learning to play an instrument etc. It's something YOU'VE thought of, something inside you that has told you that it would be good for you to do it. On the other hand, 'Just say yes' is bowing down to social pressures – going to that birthday party or family dinner because someone else tells you that you have to. You don't. If you're feeling like you can't because you want to be alone and you need to sit in silence while you're anxiety passes, 'Just say no.' If you think you'll feel worse the next day if you go to that party, then bin it. Put your feet up. The key is to try and get better. Doing something you don't feel like doing may in fact make you worse. When I used to find myself with spare time and I didn't use it productively, I'd beat myself up about it. Nowadays I've got better at reminding myself to enjoy the blank space, embrace the quietness; it may not come around again for a while. In the past, I tried to force entertainment or the next business idea that'll make me millions into any spare time I had and the consequent failure to succeed got me down, really down. I punished myself for not using that precious time productively. That negative reaction to 'just one of those days' can give birth to 'just one of those days' tomorrow and so on and so on, until you're caught in a web of depression that you can't get out of. The truth is that sometimes you need a breather so your brain can build up the energy to be productive later on. Don't bully yourself. Put the kettle on, put your feet up and read a book. Tomorrow is a new day.

Having said that, don't make a habit of excluding yourself from social situations or sitting on your arse for days, just remember there's nothing wrong with taking time out if you feel you need to rest and look after your brain. You have to listen to the signals.

After preaching about what works for me and trying to give advice, I have to tell you that I haven't miraculously been turned on my head and had the depression and anxiety shaken out of me. Clinically it's not there any more, but it still rises up and reminds me that it's lurking in the shallow depths of my brain pool, eyes popping up like an alligator waiting for me to make the wrong choice and snap me up. I have to tell the full story and admit that I still suffer from time to time. This week I've been feeling pretty down and haven't been able to focus. In comparison to last week, I have a lack of energy that I feel as soon as I wake up in the morning. I feel lonely.

I feel sad about the world. I have no self esteem. I've hated myself. It really is a roller coaster, up and down. I've been caught in a negative current but I've learnt to go with it and I know it'll pass. I can already feel it passing. Maybe that's it; maybe that's what keeps me from drowning. Maybe I fought too hard against the current in the past and that's what dragged me under. Maybe I put too much pressure on myself to succeed. Working hard to achieve the 'normal' life will surely make someone ill, if that's not what they actually want or they are defaulting to it because they don't know what they do want. Ironically, nowadays I do want a normal life but, back then, I didn't. I wanted it extraordinary because I couldn't see the beauty in the ordinary. I'm on a constant journey to try and figure out who I am and what I want. Sometimes I feel like my soul and spirit don't belong in this body or this time or this place and I find it very hard to scope the millions of life choices and pick the right one. I'm a floater, a drifter, and today's society doesn't allow that. It's not a practical way to be and maybe that's why, in the past, I've felt that I haven't been able to fit in. Now, I'm not trying to fit in any more, I'm just happy to be alive and I really do enjoy life more than I ever did – a beer, a cuddle, a walk, a Lion bar, a conversation, a shower and, most importantly, I cherish every single second with the ones that I love.

I don't think I'll ever be one of those people who seem to glide effortlessly through life and are always bursting with energy and happiness. I guess I'm someone who has experienced depression due to my type of brain, my life situations and personal choices, and I have to work very hard to avoid that experience again. Who knows, tomorrow I may fall back into depression? I believe there are too many variables in life to be able to pinpoint exactly what makes us depressed. That's why medically there's still so much unknown about mental health and so much to learn about why we humans think the way we do. The only thing you can do is keep going – just keep trudging through the bullshit because, even though you may lose a few shoes in it along the way, you'll be able to get across eventually and, when you do, you can look back at them shit shoes and know that you managed it the best you could. If you manage to get to old age and live long enough that old age is the thing that kills you, you are lucky. Everything else in between is a bonus.

I think I now finally realise how lucky I am just to be alive. I've learnt to go back to the very basics. It's survival that's most important and all the other things in life are luxuries – this computer I'm typing on is a luxury, the tea I'm sipping is a luxury, just waking up in the morning is a luxury. I try not to look too far ahead any more – just far enough so I can maintain today's happiness for as long as possible. You can't guarantee a future of happiness. You never know what's around the corner. All those chestnuts you've been saving up can be washed out in a second and you'll be back with the only things you have that are guaranteed: your skin and your ability to love.

My experience of depression has gone from naivety about the power of it, to a happy medium where we both exist and now, finally, I am technically free from it. I've been taken off the list. Normal brain. That wasn't supposed to happen to me. I was sure I had a future of mental struggle. I guess I still do, we all do, but I never thought I would be in control of it and now I know I am, to a certain extent. I can't predict my mental health but I have a chance to direct it. I used to think that I would be better off dead. I'm not. You're not. None of us is. We have the most precious thing on this beautiful planet and that is life. Keep going, look after it and, no matter what happens, eventually the light will shine through. The saying 'What doesn't kill you makes you stronger' has real meaning to me now. My experience gives literal meaning to that saying for me. The fucker didn't kill me, but it has made me stronger.

Letter to my Younger Self

Dear Tim,

I bet you would have never thought you'd write a book and have it published, would you? I double bet you wouldn't believe me if I told you it was about your life and the experiences you're going though right now. I'm pretty certain you wouldn't believe me if I told you that nowadays you wake up every morning looking forward to making your future a happy one. And you definitely wouldn't believe me if I told you that you've started piano lessons.

I know that any sort of happiness seems unreachable to you right now but you have to believe me that it is. You have to believe me because I'm here alive writing this and I'm happy. One day you were so happy and laughed so hard that you actually pissed yourself a little bit. You want to feel that excitement and warmth again, don't you? You do find a way out of this misery. Right now you've only scratched the surface of searching for a way out. I'm not going to lie and say it will be easy because it was a slog but, my god, was it worth it.

You have to survive. Strength in survival is rewarded with a new day, a new day that has endless opportunities – opportunities to grow, opportunities to explore this amazing playground of life. If you can't do it for yourself, do it for Frank. Frank is your son, by the way. Yeah, you have a son. How amazing is that? He's taught you more than you'll ever know. He brings so much joy to your life – more than you'll ever be able to imagine. You have to be here to pay him back for that.

Trust me, I am you. I am living your future and it's worth every second of the pain you feel right now. Learn to look after yourself, it's important. Once you do that, you'll learn to love yourself and, once you've achieved that, you'll learn the best lesson of all and that is to love others.

One last thing, whatever you do, make sure you leave your medication in your backpack on 11 September 2013. Something pretty special happens.

Tim x

AFTERWORD

During and after the show we received so many emails from people who had watched us and related to my story in some way. Here's a selection of some of those emails – in some cases I've changed names or details to protect privacy, but they are otherwise true to what was originally sent and I'm forever grateful to the people who got in touch and shared their own experiences.

---------- Message ----------
Subject: Fake It 'Til You Make It

Dear Tim,

I've never done this before. I wanted to write to you to say thank you. I came to see the show last week and it's not left my head since. I can't explain how it's made me feel. All I can say is that it's made me turn a real corner with my own life, and taught me to be more honest with myself and open with others about my own illness, both physical and mental. I've suffered from chronic fatigue syndrome and depression for nearly two years now, both of which feed each other, causing extremely low moods and consistent thoughts of death – or rather not living – and seeing the show has made me for the first time reach out for help about my mental illness. I can't tell you how much I think it's already making me feel better, sharing what's wrong, not suffering in silence. Without your show and your story I wouldn't have had the courage to do that. Thank you so much for sharing it with the world. It seems dramatic to say that it's changed my life, but it might just have done that.

So, yeah. I met you after the show and I didn't really know what to say, other than 'Thank you', with my eyes and cheeks a bit damp. So this is me saying thank you again.

I just wish I could come and see the show again at the Soho Theatre. I've never been so personally affected by anything in my life.

Best wishes,

Ewan White

---------- Message ----------

Subject: Thank you

Hi both,

Just wanted to say thanks for Latitude. It was just beautiful and might just have been the most impactful art in any form I have ever seen. Yes, that good. And that's from someone who saw The Icicle Works in Slough in 1984 and had a can of beer with the band backstage afterwards with my mate Steve.

I was in the half of the audience that was in tears by the end. And we men aren't supposed to cry, especially at 56. But fuck that. What are we teaching our sons if we don't express our emotions?

In terms of how Fake It has impacted me, I talked honestly with my mate Jordan about how I had been feeling at work that afternoon (I was playing bingo with the depression symptoms as you held them up and was doing quite well in a game you don't want to win) and went to the doctor the following Tuesday. I'm stressed, not depressed, thankfully. Jordan thinks you will save lives and he's right.

I'd had a previous thing happen (not in the same league as yours Tim) and hadn't considered that it could be a chronic condition. I thought I'd just got some perspective and got fitter to get over it and it was in the past.

I'll briefly share my story using email because a song or dance from me would just confuse you.

I myself work in a corporate environment so I understood Tim's presentation. I nodded knowingly as he spoke, then laughed nervously when I clicked it was a parody. Yes, we really do say that stuff. I also remember the feeling of being on autopilot making a presentation while your head is spinning, feeling dizzy and not knowing if I could continue. It happened to me in Dubai. Some months later it all came to a head and I just started crying in my office so I got in the car and drove until I reached the coast. I stopped then, not wanting to be a complete drama queen. I'm a man after all.

The truth is that my wife then and I were both going through similar things separately so neither was able to help the other. That's my analysis, she may think I'm an almighty twat who happened to be depressed or stressed. Anyway, I got a counsellor, a personal trainer and a new job (old boss was a bell-end and source of stress). Within a year I was stones lighter and single and over a year on from that

I'm better than ever, living around the corner from my lovely girlfriend. I see the kids regularly and we do things like Latitude together.

About a month ago work started getting to me again and I started losing sleep. I was getting irritable and tired at work. You know the kind of thing. Latitude was a much needed break and then my mate suggested we check you out. If he hadn't, we wouldn't have talked about it afterwards, gone to the docs and sorted a plan to make it easier for me and everyone at work. It's that simple.

My girlfriend is away at the moment but we have spoken about the play and we'll be coming to see it together in Soho (I have to if I want to know what Bryony makes for breakfast on consecutive mornings). I've spoken to my girlfriend quite a lot about my 'mini-meltdown' but this is a good way to have further talks so she knows what she is getting in to.

I've also said to my management team that I was losing sleep over work and had been to the doctors about it. They might have thought I was mad. I'm not, just stressed. That's prompted other conversations about how we are all coping at work. This stuff can't be taboo so thank you for prompting it.

Finally, hopefully this will make you laugh Tim. As the performance started (and I had no clue what to expect) my immediate reaction was "Oh, Bryony is expecting and I bet that's a male model in his underwear. Couldn't she find a less manly actor?"

Exactly.

Facing your fears head on in front of an audience in your bloody underwear is one of the bravest things I've ever seen anyone do. That's got to be closer to whatever manly is than Popeye.

I wish you and your family nothing but good things and if I can help in any small way, I'd be delighted to.

Thank you so much for doing it. You have already helped me so much you brilliant, talented, brave, wonderful life-savers.

T.

---------- Message ----------
Subject: The show

Hi there guys,

Firstly I want to say how amazing the show was and I hope that it will be a big success.

I thought that I'd write just to say that I also suffer from clinical depression and have done for the past 7 years. It's been a hard time for me and also partners that have been in my life, it's such an amazing thing that u have here if only I could find some of like you bryony who wants to understand and help, none of my exs actually could deal with it and all have left me because of it.

Your show help me Tim to see the light as the end of the tunnel (where ever that may be or not). Everything that was done during the show was me, I used to be a performer and then one day I lost it and I haven't been on the stage since. I just wanted to say that Tim you have inspired me to sort my set out again and get back on the stage.

The main thing which rang true with me was the hiding of the face because I do that too, I hide behind my sunglasses so I don't have to look into people's eyes and they can't see me.

Tim I think it was amazing how u laid yourself bare on stage and expressed all the emotions, I still find it hard to express anything to anyone because of people not understanding but with your show I believe that will change.

Thank you for showing me that anyone can do it

I loved the duvet song actually made me cry because I understood every single word

I wish u both the very best for Edinburgh

Kindest regards

Mark

---------- Message ----------

Subject: thanks

Hey guys,

Just wanted to say thanks for last night. I started blubbing at the end so my boyfriend ushered me out, only for me to look over and realize he was crying too.

We went outside and he told me about having depression for a year – ending just before we met – self-harming and self-medicating with alcohol and weed and going through shit days at work feeling like he had that cloud thing Tim had on his head and going to the toilets to cry. He'd never told ANYONE about it before.

If that's just me and him, who else did it strike a chord for? Maybe someone else spoke up to their girlfriend about it.

Well done + thanks,

Sheila x

---------- Message ----------

Subject: Last night

Sceptical about shows that deal with mental health because usually made from positions of incredible privilege

Greatly enjoyed the show last night and QnA anyway but never imagined I'd be emailing you

Got home to find out my dad had tried to take his own life again but first episode in 5 years. Complications and details are incidental but key thing is I sort of understood after seeing your show.

Mum properly talked to me this morning about it unlike in past – she almost told the story of your show and it was a good reference point for me to understand him and also her (she doesn't want to tell anyone) – I was getting upset at my desk after and feeling helpless and in front of me your leaflet with mind's number was right in front of me. Got the ball rolling as a result with help – he never accepted his diagnosis in the past. Hopefully this time he will.

I always ask if theatre can really bring about social change. Apparently it can.

Thank you a lot

Rich

---------- Message ----------

Subject: Hi

Dear Bryony and Tim,

I wanted to let you know I loved your show tonight. Loved it. My wife and kids did too. So great for Naomi and Billy to have seen something so true and funny and real about depression. They know their Dad has suffered from it and I think what you did was demystify and humanise the whole subject. I asked Billy – who's 13 – how he'd describe it and he said 'comic realism'. Bloody heck.

I am copying this to Holly Florentina who was raving – quite rightly – about your work, Bryony. And sent me a flyer so I didn't miss tonight. Holly, thank you.

And also to Simon Bogart and Jess Greaves, two magnificent friends who are leading a movement to destigmatize depression in the workplace. Tim, I mentioned this to you. Simon and Jess, all I can say is go to the show, immediately. And tell everyone in your group! It's brilliant.

At the end Bryony talked about the 'tribe' of people who have suffered and/or been touched by depression and are getting on with it. I certainly feel part of it. And there are thousands like us. I think we should wear one of those

Japanese dolls round our necks and carry an eggbeater. That should get depression talked about in the workplace.

Thanks again. We can't stop talking about the show. And don't intend to. . .

With love,

W

---------- Message ----------

Subject: Thank you

Hello Tim and Bryony,

Words can't really articulate how beautiful an act you produce for an audience. Thank you so much for opening up your lives to us and sharing your story. So many of my friends deal with depression and your show has had what I'm sure will be a lasting affect on them. I thank you also for the strength of your honesty, the great emotional intelligence, and the beautiful love and care you have not just for each other but for your audience as well. I was deeply moved. Thank you again for reminding us that none of us do this alone, we are all still here for each other and we happily share the load.

John

---------- Message ----------

Subject: Thanks so much

Dear Bryony and Tim,

I am a 17 year old boy from London.
I recently watched your show Fake It 'Til You Make It at the Edinburgh Fringe Festival and it ignited in me a feeling much like that of euphoria. Watching your story on manic depression related so much to my life that I almost had the urge to leave the theatre just to not have to think about it anymore. However I'm glad I stayed because seeing how much you went through and how brilliant you turned out and how absolutely amazing it is that you worked through it because of love for each other gave me so much hope I burst into tears. You have both inspired me so much I cannot even begin how to thank you. Since watching your show I have been diagnosed with manic depression and have told all my family and friends but I feel your show is the strand of hope I have of beating it and I honestly feel I can. Thank you so much for what you have done for me and I wish you both the very best for your future because you deserve it. (Also, loved the dancing).
   Ricky Carnavon

---------- Message ----------

Subject: Re: Fake it till you make it and me

Hi Ricky,

Thanks so much for your email. Sorry for the delayed response.

We are in our lounge in Edinburgh and both feel very moved by your email. I am very glad you have been to the doctors AND that you have a support network of friends and family to tap into. Don't be ashamed, just make sure you ALWAYS have someone to talk to.

We love the dancing too!

Much love

Bry and Tim xx

---------- Message ----------

Subject: Fake It Till You Make It

Hey kids,

You said at the end of the show, to get in touch if we wanted to, so I decided I would.

I saw your show tonight and just wanted to say thank you. I feel like I have more or less been battling with depression since I was 16. That's literally half my life. I've always tried to brush it aside thinking you just gotta take the good with the bad but even though it's progressively got worse (crying a lot, the helplessness, the anxiety), I've always put off doing anything about it.

Funnily enough, today, before your show, I booked an appointment with a psychologist for next week. And I was in two minds about it because today I felt somewhat better than the last four days of sleeplessness and anxiety. But having watched your show and hearing you, Tim, talk about the 8-year battle and what you went through, I know that even though right now I am OK, overall I am not. So I am sticking with the appointment and hopefully onwards to better things.

So thank you again, I am sure you've heard this a lot already, but your show was helped me take that plunge and really get some help for this.

love to you both,

David

---------- Message ----------
Subject: Fake it til you make it

Dear Bryony and Tim,

I had the absolute pleasure of seeing your show last night and hearing you speak at the q and a after. I just wanted to thank you so much for this gift and express just how grateful I am that you both had the courage to create something so beautiful out of so much pain. I've suffered from severe depression most of my life, as have both my parents. My dad actually committed suicide when I was very young. Last night I found myself wishing he could have been there with me to share this experience because it's honestly one of the most inspiring and life affirming things I've ever witnessed. As you both know, mental illness has a way of isolating and disconnecting you from your fellow man but last night as I sat in an audience full of people who've been touched by illness and were as moved by your piece as I was I felt for the first time like I was part of a community. I've never been so happy.

In short; thank you both for being the beautiful, extraordinary human beings that you are and I hope you both come back to Australia because I'll most definitely see anything you do in the future.

Best wishes

Ben Archer

PS Tim I most certainly understand feeling incredibly depressed in moments of happiness and euphoria. It's a mystery to us all.

---------- Message ----------

Subject: Thank you!!!

Hi Bryony and Tim,

I am writing to you as I saw your incredible show this morning!

Over the last few months I have started seeing someone who I recently found out suffers from depression so this show really struck a chord with me, and has actually made me feel more proactive and capable of helping and supporting him in a more active way. I have a couple of friends who suffer from depression and so I have some understanding of it, but seeing the show has really opened my eyes in a different way. You have encouraged me to do some real research into what depression actually is, get a better understanding of the symptoms and different types of treatment.

So basically, I think you are both wonderful and I want to thank you for being brave enough and honest enough to make a hugely moving and entertaining piece of work that really is going to help change the world!

Thank you and I wish you all the very best with the rest of the tour, and your little one :)

Huge love,

Jo xxx

---------- Message ----------

Subject: Greetings

Hi Bryony & Tim,

I saw your show last night and just wanted to say how brilliant I thought it was. I went in there pretty blind as my girlfriend had got the tickets but I was really blown away, so thank you both for the honesty and integrity you put into it.

The parallels/similarities I drew with my own life and relationships (past and present) were many and if nothing else, it's comforting to know that in your own head you can feel fucking mental, but other people do too.

Good luck with the rest of the shows.

Jamie

---------- Message ----------

Subject: Thanks for Fake It 'Til You Make It

Dear Tim and Bryony,

I just saw this evening's performance of Fake It 'Til You Make It.

On two separate occasions I have visited a GP with regard to depression when I was "feeling down". The first (many years ago), a rather horrible experience involving a multiple choice questionnaire and a hasty prescription for antidepressants that I didn't take; the second (more recently) a much more positive experience that left me convinced that I do not suffer from depression.

Regardless, I have still been in a state of confusion as to what depression is. I find this difficult, not only because I have had periods of time where I have felt like I may be depressed, but also because I have friends who have suffered from depression of varying degrees and I struggle to understand what they are going through.

I can't accurately put into words all the things I gained from watching your show, but it has truly helped my understanding of mental illness, and has improved my willingness to, and confidence in helping those who I am able to in the future.

I wanted to take the time to thank you for your dedication putting your show together, and performing it. What you are doing is both admirable and inspirational, I wish you both well on your continuing tour and hope that others can gain as much from your story as I have, if not more.

All the best,

Danny

Acknowledgements

First and foremost, I want to say the biggest thanks to Bryony. You woke me up. I love you and I always will, even your dinosaur feet.

I also want to thank the following people who made this book possible. My editor Briony (confusing isn't it?) made me chill out and just write. So my second thanks goes to her. Thanks Briony for being a calm voice through this whole process and for encouraging me to write with no hesitation. Thanks also to Vero and everyone else at Hodder, what a lovely bunch. Big thanks to Cath too, super-agent.

Massive thanks to Jo, without you this would basically have just been a book of muddled thoughts, thank you for unwinding my spaghetti brain.

Mum, Dad and siblings, thank you for your unconditional love and making me smile whenever I think of you.

Bexy, thank you, mate, for being there while I wrote. I needed you. Good friends are important and I'm lucky enough to have a lot of them, you know who you all are, thanks for not moaning because I haven't written out your names individually!

I feel I have to thank every single person involved in Fake It 'Til You Make It, from the Kickstarter supporters to the audience members, thank you for being kind, supportive and enthusiastic. You all made it the life changing experience it really was.

Finally, thank you to my boy Frank. Thank you for giving me purpose.